FLORET FARM'S

Cut Flower
Garden

FLORET FARM'S

Cut Flower Garden

GROW, HARVEST & ARRANGE STUNNING SEASONAL BLOOMS

ERIN BENZAKEIN

WITH JULIE CHAI

PHOTOGRAPHS BY MICHÈLE M. WAITE

CHRONICLE BOOKS

SAN FRANCISCO

Library of Congress Cataloging-in-Publication Data
Names: Benzakein, Erin, author. | Chai, Julie, author.
Title: Floret Farm's Cut Flower Garden / by Erin Benzakein with Julie Chai.
Description: San Francisco, California : Chronicle Books, [2017]
Identifiers: LCCN 2016011482 | ISBN 9781452145761 (hardcover : alk. paper)
Subjects: LCSH: Cut flowers. | Flower arrangement.
Classification: LCC SB405 .B495 2017 | DDC 635.9/66–dc23 LC record
 available at http://lccn.loc.gov/2016011482

Manufactured in China

Design by Anne Kenady

10 9 8 7 6 5 4 3 2 1

Chronicle books and gifts are available at special quantity discounts to corporations, professional associations, literacy programs, and other organizations. For details and discount information, please contact our corporate/premiums department at corporatesales@chroniclebooks.com or at 1-800-759-0190.

Chronicle Books LLC
680 Second Street
San Francisco, California 94107
www.chroniclebooks.com

For Grammy, who planted the love of
flowers in my heart.

CONTENTS

INTRODUCTION

Growing up, I spent time every summer with my grandparents in the country in eastern Washington. They lived in a small town that was surrounded on all sides by wheat fields, onion farms, and a sky that went on forever. The days were hot and slow and wonderful—nothing like our busy life back home in Seattle.

When my grandparents were at work during the day, my sister and I would head down to my great grandparents' place. There we played in the creek, drank as much soda pop as we wanted, and spent endless hours exploring the fields and forests surrounding their house. My great-grandmother, Grammy, was something of a legend—or at least her garden was. I'd hear stories of how she'd built her first garden, one wheelbarrow load of soil at a time, on completely barren land in the desert of Nevada. Back in the day, she poured her heart and soul into that little plot, and everyone who had known her then would smile as they recalled her property with the blue morning glory-covered fences and flowerbeds overflowing with gorgeous blooms.

By the time Grammy came into my life, that little oasis was just a magical memory. She had moved north to be closer to family, leaving behind her beloved garden. Grammy was bedridden by then, and on those long, hot days, I would lie beside her as she told me tales of her flowers. She often sent me outside with scissors to pick her a bouquet. While her new little plot was nothing like her old garden, there were still a few treasures to be found if you dug around long enough. I'd collect leggy snapdragons, bug-chewed tea roses, and handfuls of cheery sweet peas that were scrambling up the porch posts.

I took my flower-picking job very seriously. After gathering a collection of slightly wilted blooms from the yard, I'd dig through Grammy's stash of old, dusty bud vases and find just the right one. Those scrappy little bouquets must have been quite the sight, but she always cooed and doted over them as if they were diamonds or fine china.

Grammy passed away the year my husband and I bought our first house. I was able to bring some of her ashes home with me and spread them in my new garden. I planted two long rows of sweet peas down the center of the plot in her memory. Those sweet peas bloomed so abundantly that I filled every room in our house with bouquets all summer long, and ended up sharing the bounty with anyone and everyone I knew.

During that abundant summer, word of our flowers got out, and someone ordered a jar of sweet peas for a friend. I'll never forget that first delivery. I nervously knocked on the stranger's door and awkwardly thrust the bouquet into her hands, not knowing exactly what to say. Surprised, she buried her face in the flowers, and within moments her eyes were filled with tears. She shared that the scent transported her back to childhood summers and a time of great happiness in her grandmother's garden. In that moment, I realized that I'd found my calling. Witnessing the profound impact that a simple bouquet could have on a person, I knew I had discovered something worth pursuing.

The following spring I replanted the vegetable garden with flowers. The winter after that, I dug up the orchard to make room for more blooms. The summer after that, my husband built me a greenhouse, and then a few more. Every season since, the garden has grown, and along with it my love for flowers.

My time is now spent growing, teaching, and sharing the beauty of flowers with people all over the world. Those first two rows of sweet peas have since turned into Floret Farm, a thriving flower farm that supplies shops, grocery stores, and florists throughout the Pacific Northwest. Attached to the garden is our bustling design studio where we create seasonal bouquets for weddings and events. The farm has also become a school, and each year we open it up to flower lovers who travel from around the globe to learn about small-scale, high-intensity flower production, and the art of natural floral design. My love for trialing and variety selection has blossomed into my mail-order seed company, which offers my favorite, tried-and-true varieties for cutting and arranging, along with a selection of my must-have tools. If someone had told me way back then that that little jar of sweet peas would have turned into this flower-filled life, I never would have believed it.

Over the course of my journey, I've heard from thousands of budding flower farmers, floral designers, and home gardeners who long to know more about how they, too, can have a life filled with flowers. From simple growing instructions to specific variety selections, basic cut flower care to seasonally based floral arranging techniques, they are hungry for more information.

The underlying philosophy of this book is that using local blooms and other materials when they're in season, at their most abundant, will give you the most luscious, beautiful bouquets. Food lovers have eagerly embraced the practice of eating what's in season, and many of the world's most respected chefs base their menus on the freshest regional ingredients they can find, with the knowledge that produce flown in from thousands of miles away, at the wrong time of year, pales in comparison to perfectly ripe treasures picked nearby, at their peak.

Consumers are demanding to know how, where, and by whom their goods are produced. Flowers are no exception. On the heels of the local food movement, the field-to-vase movement is continuing its meteoric rise in popularity. High-end florists are now seeking locally grown blooms, and working to grow some of their own material to supplement what they source from wholesale outlets. Eco-conscious couples are choosing seasonal flowers for their wedding bouquets. Many young farmers are looking to flowers as a viable crop to cultivate. And home gardeners everywhere are itching to tuck a bed or two of flowers, just for cutting, into their existing landscapes.

Each season has its stars. Early spring welcomes fragrant narcissus, showy tulips, and many types of unique flowering bulbs. Late spring is filled with blooming branches, heady sweet peas, and big billowy peonies. As summer arrives, with it come garden roses, lilies, and all of the cheerful warm weather lovers such as zinnias, cosmos, and dahlias. Autumn ushers in textural elements like grasses, grains, and pods that pair beautifully with sunflowers and showy chrysanthemums. In winter, the abundance continues indoors with pots of forced amaryllises and paperwhites, and evergreen garlands and wreaths. By looking to

nature for cues, flower lovers can savor the best of the bounty by enjoying each bloom while it's at its peak.

The beauty of planning around the seasons is that it doesn't matter where you live or what your climate is like. As soon as you learn the general timing of your last frost date in spring and your first frost date in autumn, you can grow an abundance of crops within those months, and possibly year-round.

There is something magical about experiencing an entire year through flowers. Because my work requires me to have a close connection to the landscape, I find I'm much more present in the moment and connected to the seasonal shifts going on around me. Once you start growing your own cutting garden and working with seasonal flowers, you'll likely notice a powerful transformation in your awareness as you tune in to the subtle, magical changes in nature.

In the pages ahead, you will find all of the information you need to start growing your own cut flowers. The book is organized into two major parts. The first digs into the basics of planning, designing, and stocking your cutting garden and includes instructions for tried-and-true techniques. The second covers detailed growing and harvesting instructions for a year's worth of beautiful blooms, along with key tasks and step-by-step projects, all organized by season.

My hope is that this book will continue the legacy that Grammy started almost a century ago in her little plot of ground. We need more people like Grammy— and the world definitely needs more flowers. Wherever you are on the garden path, I invite you to join me and countless others around the globe in cultivating more beauty with seasonal blooms.

Happy growing!

BAS

ICS

FOUNDATION

Unlike a mixed border or showy flower bed that functions to provide a pretty and perfect display, a cutting garden's primary job is to produce a bounty of cut blooms all season long. While a cutting patch is beautiful in its own right, the flowers that fill it are there to be harvested, not left on the plants for garden decoration. This can take some getting used to because, as gardeners, we've been conditioned to resist the urge to clip from our blooming plants, and instead leave them to put on a show outdoors. But once you experience the pleasure of harvesting armloads of flowers right outside your door, your approach to growing them will quickly change.

Where I live, in Washington's Skagit Valley, the climate is temperate with a wet spring; a mild, dry summer; a cool, damp autumn; and a cold, rainy winter. This book highlights how we grow in our region, so you may need to adjust the timing of certain tasks depending on where you live. I've made the information as universal as possible, so any adjustments for your own climate should be straightforward. But feel free to consult with your local nursery if you're unsure.

Here at Floret we swear by the steps outlined here. I've broken the process into three major sections: creating a plan, putting your plan into action, and mastering important techniques. Follow this approach, and your cutting garden will overflow with blooms in no time.

17

Planning & Getting Started

For our two-acre farm, it generally takes me a few weeks to plot out the entire year's production schedule, and I never regret the investment once the season is under way. (For a home gardener, this process might take only a few afternoons.) While it may feel daunting to consider so much information when designing and stocking your cutting garden, the more time you spend on planning up front, the better your end results will be.

ASSESS & DEFINE YOUR SITE

Before planning your cutting garden on paper, it's important to know what you're working with. This includes how much space you have to grow in and what kind of sunlight it receives during the day. You'll want to position your cutting garden in as sunny a spot as possible—nearly all of the plants listed in this book prefer full sun, meaning a minimum of 6 hours a day, unless otherwise noted—with the best soil you have available or can create. Ideally, this spot would be away from standing water and large root systems, such as those from mature trees, that could compete with your plants. Not every gardener has a spot this prime, but aim for the best location you can manage. If your plot gets less than full sun, I recommend sticking with plants that thrive in shade, like foxglove, columbine, and hellebores, or annual plants that prefer cooler weather, like bells of Ireland, larkspur, and sweet peas. Once you've chosen your site, mark the corners of the plot so you don't lose track of where it'll be. Then measure the perimeter and record it in a special notebook or journal that you keep just for the garden.

PERFORM A SOIL TEST

Taking a soil test will help you better understand what's going on underground. While this step is the most often overlooked, it's also one of the most important keys to a cut flower grower's success. This comprehensive test costs about $50, depending on the lab you send it to, and it takes about a week or two to get results. When the test comes back, it will include a detailed report on your garden's soil, including what trace minerals it's lacking and what types of amendments (such as bonemeal, lime, kelp, or fertilizer blends) you can add to remedy any problems.

To prepare the test, use a large spade to dig down roughly 1 foot (30 cm). Remove a few tablespoons of soil from the bottom of the hole, then place them in a

quart-sized jar. Repeat this process at several other spots in your plot, so that you get evenly spaced samples from your entire plot, until the jar is full. Send this sample to a soil lab for testing (see "Resources," page 304, for recommended labs).

In my many years as a landscape designer and flower farmer, I've seen countless problems stem from basic soil deficiencies. I test any new garden plot I tend, heed the advice of the soil specialists, and add all of the recommended amendments suggested by the lab results. Plants, like people, need the proper minerals and vitamins to thrive. Putting a little extra effort in on the front end will pay off in the long run.

DESIGN YOUR PLOT

With measurements in hand, it's time to pull out the graph paper and start designing your plot. Unlike traditional flower beds that have curves and mixed plantings, the cutting garden should be set up with production and efficiency in mind—this means narrow, rectangular spaces that are easy to tend and harvest. Choose a bed width that allows you to reach the center when standing on either of the long sides, and establish permanent pathways between beds, not only for access, but also to make it easier to plan your plot on paper. At Floret, our growing beds are 48 inches (122 cm) wide, so we can easily reach into the center and harvest from any point, with 24-inch (61-cm) paths between beds, and a generous 4-foot (1.2-m) path down the center of the plot. A large center path isn't necessary if you are short on space.

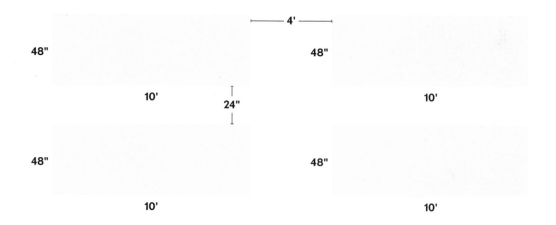

DO THE MATH

Once you have your beds and paths penciled into the plan, the next step is to calculate how many plants can fit into each bed. From there you can select what varieties to include and figure out how many seeds of each to order.

When growing flowers for cutting, your goal is twofold: to grow as many blooms as you can in the space you have, and to grow the longest stems possible, since they provide the greatest versatility for arranging (and are thus the most appealing to buyers). We space seedlings quite tightly, which allows us to grow more and results in vigorous vertical growth.

When I first started growing, I followed traditional flower gardening advice and gave each plant ample room to spread out, with just 1 or 2 rows per 48-inch (122-cm) bed. But I was constantly battling weeds, and I never had enough room in my limited space to fit in everything I wanted to grow. So, after much trial and error, I finally landed on a system that works well: I call it small-scale, high-intensity flower production. We space all annuals closely in one of three planting grids depending on their ultimate size:

6-by-6 inch (15-by-15 cm): Best for crops that have a very upright form, or have single, non-branching stems, like plumed celosia (such as Pampas Plume Mix) and cabbage, this spacing results in 7 or 8 rows per 48-inch (122-cm) wide bed.

9-by-9 inch (22-by-22 cm): This is the most common spacing of all, which works for just about any annual cut flower crop, and results in 5 rows per 48-inch (122-cm) wide bed.

12-by-12 inch (30-by-30 cm): Bulkier growers that produce a much larger volume of foliage and tend to branch out quite a bit—like amaranth, brain celosia (such as 'Kurume Orange Red'), and false Queen Anne's lace—work best in this spacing, which results in 4 rows per 48-inch (122-cm) wide bed.

Using this production method, it's easy to figure out how many plants you can fit in each bed. Simply decide what spacing you'll use, and create the appropriate grid for the length and width of your beds. For example, if your bed is 48 inches (122 cm) wide and 10 feet (3 m) long, as shown in the chart on page 21, and you're planting with 9-inch (22-cm) square spacing, you can fit 65 plants. You can grow an enormous amount of flowers in even the tiniest plot this way.

DECIDE WHAT TO ORDER

While you may want to order everything in the catalogs that's listed as being good for cutting, such a scattershot approach will only leave you overwhelmed and without adequate material for every season to get you through a full year. I like to review the past year's garden journal, which has notes about what performed well, what I noted that I wanted to decrease, and also what I raved about in friends' gardens. These insights help me decide what to grow in the coming year. If you're a new grower, I encourage you to adopt the following approach from the start: your goal is to have (1) a good mix that includes foliage and flowers, as well as tried-and-true and experimental bloomers, and (2) plants that provide material in each season.

One of the biggest newbie mistakes is selecting only pretty blooms, and not having any greenery to mix them with—and it's hugely frustrating to plant your entire patch with fifty different blooming varieties in spring, only to run out of foliage to mix with them by late summer and have nothing to cut in autumn or winter. After many years of experience, I've found that the perfect ratio is planting roughly half of the garden with mainstay foliage and plants I like to use as fillers (plants that are used in arrangements for their foliage and seedpods), including amaranth, bells of Ireland, and scented geranium, to provide a steady stream of material that will become the base of all arrangements. I set aside the other half for the ultra-showy flowers that bloom in different seasons and are sure to thrive in my climate.

A NOTE ABOUT PLANT NOMENCLATURE

As you begin planning your flower garden, it's important to understand plant nomenclature. All plants have botanical names that are unique, so that there's no confusion about which plant is being referred to. In many cases, these names include a genus, species, and variety, if there is one. A botanical name looks like this: *Fagus sylvatica* 'Tricolor'.

Most plants also have common names; these are terms that many people know them by, and they may differ from their botanical names. For example, *Fagus sylvatica* 'Tricolor' is also known as a tricolor beech tree. In some cases, confusion can arise with common names, since a single plant may have several common names, and several plants may be known by the same common name.

In this book, we list common names in cases where it's unlikely the plant would be mistaken for something else. Where further clarification may be helpful, we also list the botanical names.

Do set aside a little corner of your plot for experimenting so you can explore new options without cutting into your garden's overall production. And when growing from seed, always order 20 percent more than you think you'll need, in case some don't germinate or seedlings get eaten by slugs.

KEY CUTTING GARDEN
PLANT TYPES

The following are the main plant types with which you can fill your cutting garden—to have material for most of the year, you'll want to grow a mix of them. What you'll choose will depend on your budget, your space, and the time you have to devote to growing and tending. They're listed in order of how easy they are to grow and how quickly they produce—annuals are the simplest and quickest, while trees require more time, space, and care.

TENDER ANNUALS are plants that you sow in early spring; they bloom mainly in summer, set seed, and die when the weather cools in autumn. Roughly 60 percent of Floret's fields are planted with annuals, and they provide the bulk of our summer flowers. This is the easiest, cheapest, and fastest group of plants to grow—perfect for beginners. The first 2 years I grew flowers, my entire garden was planted solely with annuals—this was a great way to get my feet wet because the investment was minimal, so I could experiment. I like to think of annuals as the cutting gardener's training wheels: they build your confidence and experience so you can branch out into the other plant types that require more of an investment.

HARDY ANNUALS are also short-lived plants; they include larkspur, love-in-a-mist, and false Queen Anne's lace, which all live less than a year. In cold climates, you plant these in early spring. In milder climates, hardy annuals can be sown in the garden in autumn—they'll form a small clump of foliage that will overwinter, and then send up flower spikes shortly before summer begins. Hardy annuals can handle some frost, and they typically flower much earlier than tender annuals, fading when the weather gets hot.

BIENNIALS are commonly overlooked for the cutting garden, but if you can master their tricky growing cycle, you'll be generously rewarded with blooms in late spring. What makes biennials such a wonderful addition is that they bridge that awkward gap between late spring and early summer when spring bulbs are spent but the first perennials have yet to bloom. Planted in late summer, biennials grow a crown of foliage that they carry through the winter, and in late spring they send up massive spikes of flowers, blooming for 6 to 8 glorious weeks; then most set seed for a new crop and die. English country favorites such as Canterbury bells, foxglove, and sweet William belong to this family of plants.

BULBS, CORMS, AND TUBERS are bold, showy plants with saturated colors, appearing like exclamation points among other plants in the garden. Generally planted in autumn or spring, depending on the variety, bulbs, corms, and tubers are slightly different in structure from each other but essentially grow the same way: they sit underground for a few months while developing roots, then push through the soil in all of their glory. Anemones, daffodils, dahlias, fritillaria, hyacinths, lilies, ranunculus, and tulips are some of my favorites in this category.

PERENNIALS are plants that typically die back to the ground when cold weather arrives but live through winter and return each spring for a number of years, gaining in size and flowering ability with each successive year. These plants generally bloom from early summer through autumn, depending on the variety, and while you can't rely only on perennials for a year's worth of material, they do provide some wonderful cutting ingredients.

VINES like clematis and hops add movement to any arrangement. They are vigorous and require little care beyond winter pruning. By tucking in a few vines along a fence or trellis, you'll have interesting tendrils and foliage to incorporate into bouquets from spring until autumn.

SHRUBS like ninebark and viburnum are a wonderful source of interesting material. Many have beautiful flowers in the spring followed by useful foliage in the summer and berries or seed cases in autumn. If purchased as small plants, they can take 3 to 5 years to grow enough to harvest. Instead of waiting that long, I buy 3- to 5-gallon (11- to 19-liter) bare-root shrubs in the winter to give myself a jump start. While these plants are pricier than annuals and require a permanent spot in the landscape, investing the time and space earlier will reward you later.

FLOWERING TREES offer some of the most dramatic cutting material of all. Branches of varieties like plums and pussy willows can be forced into flower indoors in late winter when you need an infusion of nature inside. During spring, cherry and hawthorn lend a framework for showstopping arrangements. If you choose fruiting varieties, late summer and autumn will give you a bounty of fruit-laden branches that add a lush look to bouquets. I highly recommend tucking in as many flowering trees as you can.

23

TAKE ADVANTAGE OF
SUCCESSION PLANTING

Here are two words that every cut flower grower needs to know: succession planting. This is essentially the process of sowing multiple, smaller sets of annual seeds a few weeks apart so that when you harvest the first set of blooms, the next set will be ready for cutting a few weeks after, followed by any other sets you sow. For annuals that don't rebloom reliably, succession planting helps ensure that you'll have a steady stream of flowers.

The first year I grew, I didn't have a clue about how to make sure I had enough flowers to last from spring into autumn. I sowed one massive wave of seeds in March, planted all of the babies after our last frost, and spent the following few months weeding, watering, and waiting. I didn't harvest anything significant until early summer, and then, in a flash, I had a greater bounty than I knew what to do with. For the next 6 weeks, I cut, bunched, and delivered as many flowers as I could manage. So much went to waste because there weren't enough hours in the day to deal with it all. By midsummer, the abundance was nearly gone, with only a small row of dahlias and amaranth still putting out blooms. In the short time my garden flowered, I had built up an excited group of customers who were eager for what I was growing. But I had to call each one of them and break the sad news that my flower season had ended—not fun at all. So, in an effort to learn from my mistake, I spent that winter figuring out how I could grow a more evenly paced flow of blooms and keep it going for many months. This meant learning about succession planting.

There are a few reasons why succession planting is so beneficial for the flower grower. One is that it spreads out planting and harvesting over a much larger window of time. I have divided our growing area into multiple quadrants so I can plant in waves without needing a bunch of extra hands. If I planted the entire garden at once, there is no way I could manage. The same applies to harvesting. Since I have multiple blocks of flowers, with their bloom time staggered throughout the season, I am able to stay on top of the cutting.

I have done a fair amount of trialing to see what can and can't be succession planted in our climate, and how many crops can be squeezed into a given season. Every climate is different, so you definitely need to experiment and fine-tune what will work for you. I have found that all annuals can be replanted at least once and often twice, usually allowing 3 to 4 weeks between plantings. Each year I get better at figuring out how to grow a continually producing crop of flowers over a long period of time. While it is still a work in progress, this intensive approach allows us to produce a huge volume in a very limited space.

During the planning phase, I put all annuals into one of three categories so that I have a sense of how many times I want to replant each crop, and can order enough seed:

"CUT AND COME AGAIN" are flowers that crank out an insane amount over a long period of time. The more you cut them, the more they bloom. Cosmos, marigolds, and zinnias fall into this category. For these, I do an early planting in spring, and a second one about a month after the first.

"MEDIUM PRODUCERS" include honeywort, larkspur, millet, and snapdragons. These are similar to the "cut and come again" group but have a shorter bloom window, so they need to be replanted at closer intervals, roughly every 3 weeks.

"ONE-HIT WONDERS" include a lot of my favorite fillers, like cress and flax, as well as Bombay celosia and single stem sunflowers. These beauties come on like wildfire and are gone in a flash. They should be replanted every 2 weeks until midsummer for a steady, uninterrupted harvest.

Your last planting should be done with enough time for flowers to appear before your first autumn frost. Your seed packet or catalog will indicate how many days a crop will need to mature, and you can use that number to work backward from the average first frost date in your climate to figure out your last planting day. My last planting for any summer or autumn bloomers that take roughly 60 days to flower is July 15.

24

MAXIMIZE SMALL SPACES

Compared to many farms, ours, at just 2 acres, is considered tiny. One of the things that brings our farm a lot of attention is that we cultivate an enormous amount of flowers on a very small piece of land. When I started growing blooms in my backyard, I grew in a plot that was about 15 feet (4.5 m) wide and 40 feet (12.2 m) long, and planted everything according to the instructions on the tag. I created narrow growing beds, gave each plant plenty of room to spread out, and left a considerable amount of good growing space unused. But as my passion grew, the small plot I was tending quickly became inadequate. I tried desperately to find more land, thinking that if I could only stretch out, I'd be able to grow more flowers, and make a business out of my budding hobby. But with two small children in tow and limited funds, I was forced to make do with what I had. When faced with the challenge of wanting more from my tiny plot, I had to think creatively. After nearly a decade of abundant growing on a postage stamp–sized farm, I've cracked the code on squeezing an amazing amount of flowers into my own garden, and teach others how to do it as well. These key practices are my go-to recommendations for maximizing any size garden, from a rooftop to a rambling backyard.

CHOOSE WISELY

Even if space is limited, it's still possible to harvest buckets of blooms by choosing the right plants. Skip varieties like single stem sunflowers that give just one flower per plant and instead focus on continual bloomers like cosmos, dahlias, and zinnias. These garden workhorses will produce dozens of flowers over a long period of time and give you plenty to harvest.

For a really small plot, such as 8 by 8 feet (2.4 by 2.4 m) or less, I recommend skipping growing trees and shrubs altogether because they require a lot of room and can take years to produce cutting material. Instead, use the space to plant annuals because they're cheap, easy to grow, and ultraproductive. I list lots of great annual choices in the plant profiles.

SPACE DENSELY

When it comes to annual flowering plants, ignore what the back of the seed packet says in terms of spacing. Plants can be grown much closer together—we grow most of our annuals 9 inches (22 cm) apart—when given properly amended soil, fertilizer, and water. This way, I am able to squeeze three to four times as many flowers into a bed as I would if I followed the seed packet recommendations.

GO VERTICAL

If space is tight, consider going up rather than out with your plantings. Vines and vinelike growers are some of the best sources for cutting material and, when grown on a trellis, require minimal ground area. For example, a row of sweet peas needs to be only 18 inches (46 cm) wide, and a narrow strip of these productive bloomers will reward you with fresh flowers every day for roughly 2 months.

USE CONTAINERS

Even if you don't have actual ground to grow in, you can plant a cutting garden in pots. I have seen many gardeners build raised beds on top of driveways, old tennis courts, and even their garage roofs to raise flowers and vegetables with great success. City dwellers can transform their patio or deck by filling a collection of large containers and wooden boxes with vines and other high-yielding plants.

Digging In

Once you have a solid plan and know what you're going to plant,
it's time to get your hands dirty.

GO ORGANIC

We manage all of our gardens organically and don't use any toxic chemicals or herbicides on the property. We rely heavily on large amounts of compost and natural fertilizers (applied according to package instructions) to promote plant health and manage insects and disease. Many experts told me that flowers couldn't be raised in this manner—they said that chemical fertilizers and pest controls were the only means to keep flowers looking as perfect as they needed to for sale. But, of course, that's not true. I won't lie—growing organically is a lot more work than using chemicals—but the results are dramatically different.

FEED YOUR SOIL

Everything begins with the soil. I have found time and time again that the universal law of "you get what you give" completely applies in the garden. While it can seem counterintuitive to pour money and time into something that you don't see, I promise you, it is worth it. I look at soil preparation as investing in the future.

Compost is the backbone of our fertility regime. With so much plant mass leaving the garden each season, I feel it's extremely important to replace as much as we take out. Compost has many benefits, the most important of which is improving soil structure and enhancing soil fertility. In our sandy soil, compost is essential in helping to retain moisture and provide adequate nutrients for optimum plant growth.

Starting with the results from the soil test, I add amendments to provide any missing minerals and recommended nutrients to the garden plot, and till

them into the soil. We ideally do this in autumn, so all of the ingredients have time to dissolve and mingle with the soil. A few weeks before planting in the spring, we dig into each bed a generous 2- to 4-inch (5- to 10-cm) layer of well-rotted compost and a good dose of organic fertilizer.

WATER WELL

Second to fertile soil, consistent water is one of the biggest keys to happy flowers. When plants are young, it's easy to keep them watered by overhead sprinklers or a water wand. But as they fill in, getting moisture past the foliage canopy and onto the soil becomes tricky.

A note about water: it's important to water often enough so that soil stays evenly moist but not soggy. Additionally, you should avoid overhead watering once the flowers start to bloom, because it can damage the flowers. Drip irrigation and soaker hoses (widely available at nurseries and garden centers) are a fantastic way to get water right to where you need it—at the root zone—using roughly 25 to 40 percent less water than an overhead sprinkler. If using soaker hoses, simply lay them where you want to water. Drip systems are sort of like Tinkertoys with assorted pieces to plug together—they're not difficult to set up, but the specifics will vary based on the system you choose, so you'll need to follow the instructions. Either way, after you've added soil amendments such as compost and fertilizer, place the irrigation lines immediately.

MANAGE WEEDS

I started growing flowers when my kids were very small. Trying to keep up with all of the garden tasks and chasing two wild little ones around proved to be impossible. In an effort to minimize one of the biggest time drains of flower growing, weeding, I invested in a bunch of landscape fabric for weed suppression in both pathways and beds. My husband created a simple template out of sheet metal, and we burned perfect plant-sized holes in the fabric at the ideal spacing. This system was so successful and easy that I now have over an acre of preburned fabric that I use each season. We pull the fabric snugly over the bed and hold it in place with metal "earth staples" that we poke directly through the fabric into the soil. We overlap each new piece of fabric with the last so

that no open gaps remain to invite unwanted weeds. Most crops are planted into the fabric and weeded only once or twice in an entire growing season. It is so much easier to wrangle extra help a few times a year to lay the fabric before planting, and to remove it at the end of the growing season, than it is to get help every week to stay on top of weeding.

Using landscape fabric isn't necessary to grow great flowers, but finding efficient ways to stay ahead of the weeds is. It is all a matter of preference. Many growers I know love the solitary chore of hoeing endless rows in the flower field. If this is the method you prefer, then by all means go for it, but be sure to invest in a lightweight collinear hoe. This special tool has a long, narrow, sharp blade angled flush with the soil surface that cuts tiny weeds off at the roots as you guide it from an upright position, so the task is easier on your body than the familiar "chopping" hoe.

Other growers who have access to large amounts of mulch are able to cover their beds in a thick layer of organic matter to suppress weeds; they then plant right through it. Rotted leaves, straw, and dry grass clippings are all wonderful choices for mulching flower-beds. Just steer clear of anything that may harbor large amounts of weed seeds, such as old hay, raw manure, or compost that was made through the cold composting method.

GET PLANTING

After you've amended your beds, laid irrigation lines, and placed landscape fabric or mulch, it's time for the best part: planting. My favorite tool for this task is a butter knife, because it's lightweight and fits perfectly into my preburned landscape fabric holes. For larger plants, a hori hori knife or small hand trowel does an excellent job.

Use the garden plan you created to space your seeds or plants, then plant seedlings so that the plant's crown is at or just slightly above the soil surface. Once plants are tucked into the ground, it is critical that they don't get stressed while they are rooting in. To ensure this, we water all new plants immediately and deeply, then give a weekly application of liquid seaweed and fish emulsion, following label instructions. This magic brew feeds the young plants and helps lessen transplant shock while also building up their immune systems for the future. I like to think that plants are a lot like people: the better they are cared for from the beginning, the healthier they'll be for life.

Essential Techniques

By mastering a few simple methods, you can maximize your plants' health and productivity in simple ways.

STARTING SEEDS 101

Starting your own seeds is a great way to get a jump on the season. It also gives you access to hundreds of specialty varieties that you won't find at your local nursery and is the most affordable way to fill a cutting garden fast. You just need to keep a few key things in mind before you start.

KNOW YOUR LAST SPRING AND FIRST AUTUMN FROST DATES

Before you go crazy sowing seeds in late winter and early spring, it's important to know just how early you can start—if in doubt, ask your local Master Gardener group or staff at a trusted nursery for the expected last frost date. Fast-growing annuals that bloom in summer (those that take less than 90 days to harvest, such as cosmos, sunflowers, and zinnias—the number of days to harvest is indicated on seed packets) shouldn't be started more than 4 to 6 weeks before the last spring frost; otherwise, they'll get too big for their growing container and have soft, weak foliage and overgrown roots. On the other hand, slow-growing plants like perennials can take a couple of weeks to germinate, so sow them indoors 10 to 12 weeks before the last spring frost date. Once you know your last frost date, check the back of each seed packet for days-to-harvest to figure out how many weeks early you can get them started indoors.

For the most part, if you want to sow successive crops after the weather has warmed in spring, you can plant until midsummer (or even early autumn in the mildest climates) in order to give them enough time to mature. It works like this: if, for example, what you're planting takes 60 days to mature, note your first autumn frost date, and count back 60 days. That would technically be the last date you could plant that crop for the season. But know that as the days get colder and shorter, plant growth slows. So, to be on the safe side and ensure that I have enough time for crops to mature, I like to count back an extra month to be sure my plants will flower and I'll have something to harvest.

CHOOSE THE RIGHT CONTAINER

You can start seeds in just about anything that holds soil and drains water, including egg cartons, old pots, and plastic cups with holes poked in the bottom. If you're reusing pots, be sure to wash them thoroughly with a 10-percent bleach-water solution to kill any lingering diseases or pathogens. But for the best results, I highly recommend recycled cell packs—the kind you see at garden centers holding 4 to 6 seedlings—from a local nursery, or new seed flats, which are basically shallow, perforated trays made specifically for growing seeds (see "Resources," page 304).

31

Flats come in numerous sizes, so choosing can be a little overwhelming. I've tested them all, and my two favorites for both annual and perennial seeds are the 72-cell and 50-cell flats. Both produce large, bulky plants that won't require repotting before it's time to transplant them into the garden. For vines, pumpkins, and sweet peas, I use 4-inch (10-cm) pots; for sweet peas, I also love root trainers (long, skinny growing containers that give vigorous roots room to develop—see "Resources," page 304).

In addition to seed flats and pots, you need drainage trays to set the containers on, as well as some type of plastic covering to keep up the humidity seeds need to germinate properly. You can often find kits that include all three components: a seed flat, drainage tray, and plastic dome. If you're in a bind, plastic wrap is an option, but you'll need to monitor your trays closely for signs of germination and remove it immediately once they break through the soil surface so that it doesn't impede growth. I strongly recommend getting a few clear acrylic lids that will fit snuggly over your seed trays and flats of pots. These maintain the humidity and high heat that will speed germination and growth significantly. See "Resources," page 304, for all of these.

USE GOOD SOIL

It's important to start plants off right with the highest-quality seed starting mix. You get what you pay for, so don't go for the cheapest option. These special blends contain the right mix of ingredients to ensure that your little seedlings get off to a good start. Be sure to check the ingredients and avoid any that contain synthetic fertilizers or bark, since young plants can be burned or stunted by either. Seed starting mix is fine and suited to tiny seeds. For varieties that have larger seeds and will be started in bigger pots, like vines and squash, use a high-quality potting soil.

PROVIDE BOTTOM HEAT

For seeds to germinate rapidly, they need to be kept warm and moist. If you have a cozy spot where you can tuck a few trays, like on top of the refrigerator or radiator, this heat will encourage seeds to sprout more quickly. But if you really get hooked on flower growing, you'll outgrow these spaces fast. Invest in a heat mat (see "Resources," page 304), specially designed for seed starting, for more consistent results.

PROVIDE PLENTY OF LIGHT

Of course, there's nothing better than having your very own greenhouse or sunroom to propagate plants in, but if you don't have this kind of space, don't worry. You can still get great results with a homemade seedling chamber, which can be as simple as a warm, indoor spot with shop lights. The first few years I grew flowers, I started all of my seeds in the basement, on shelves, under lights. For very little money, you can pick up a few shop lights that are available at just about any hardware store. Hang them from some inexpensive chains, and you're in business. To give plants the full spectrum of light needed to thrive, be sure to get one cool and one warm bulb (they'll be labeled as such) for each fluorescent light ballast. Suspend the lights a few inches above your seedlings and put them on a timer, making sure to give plants 14 to 16 hours of light a day. As the plants get taller, be sure to keep raising the lights so they are 2 to 3 inches (5 to 7 cm) above the tallest plant.

DIRECT SEED

I start roughly 90 percent of my seeds inside the greenhouse. This gives me a jump on the season, since I can set out larger plants once the weather has warmed. It also helps cut down on weeds, since I'm planting established plants that have a better chance of contending with the weeds and crowding or shading them out.

But not all plants need this special treatment. Many gardeners direct seed—that is, they sow seeds directly in the ground outside. I consider a few floral candidates worthy of being sown this way, including fast-growing summer annuals like grains, grasses, sunflowers, and zinnias, which all sprout within a few days of seeding. Also, many hardy annuals, like bells of Ireland, larkspur, and love-in-a-mist, resent transplanting and actually do best when sown directly into the soil.

Direct seeding can be done by hand, but if you have more than a few tiny rows to do, use a walk-behind seeder, like the Earthway (see "Resources," page 304), to make this chore a snap. This handy tool digs a furrow, drops the seeds into it, and covers them all with soil while you walk at a normal pace. With it, you can direct seed a 25-foot (7.6-m) row in less than 30 seconds.

GROWING FROM SEED IN TRAYS OR POTS, STEP BY STEP

1 Moisten your potting soil until it's thoroughly damp, but not dripping wet.

2 Fill seed flats and/or pots to the top with soil, tapping them firmly against the table as you go so that the soil settles in and there are no air pockets trapped in the tray cells or pots.

3 Label the tray or pot with the name of the variety you plan to sow and the date planted.

4 Refer to the seed packet for planting depth; a general rule of thumb is to plant the seed twice as deep as its longest side. Make a hole for the seed in each cell or pot using your finger, a pencil, or a dibbler (a tool that makes holes for seed).

5 Drop 1 or 2 seeds into each hole.

6 Add a light dusting of seed starting mix—or, for larger seeds, add about ¼ inch (0.6 cm) of potting soil—over the surface, making sure to cover all of the seeds.

7 Set freshly sown trays or pots in a plastic tub with an inch (2.5 cm) of water in the bottom, and let the trays soak up the water from below. Remove once the soil surface is evenly moist; don't let trays or pots sit in water for more than an hour.

8 Cover the trays or pots with a clear plastic dome and set on a 70°F (21°C) heat mat or in a warm corner of the house. Seeds will usually sprout before you need to water again, but check the soil for moistness after 2 to 3 days and bottom water again if it's dry.

9 Check the trays or pots daily. Once the seeds have sprouted, remove the plastic dome lids and move the trays or pots to a spot with bright light such as a sunroom or greenhouse, or under fluorescent lights. The very first leaf or leaves that appear are called cotyledons; those that appear after are known as true leaves. Bottom water until true leaves appear.

10 Check seedlings daily, and when the soil starts to become dry (which could be every day or two), water with a very gentle spray from a hose or watering can. As young plants grow, they need to be fed. Add a small amount of liquid seaweed and fish emulsion, following the label, to your watering can and drench plants weekly.

11 When seedlings begin to outgrow their trays or pots, at about 2 inches (5 cm) tall, repot them into larger containers. Or, if the weather is warm enough (after all danger of frost has passed), begin transitioning them outside.

12 It's important to "harden off" young plants before putting them out in the garden; otherwise, they will be shocked by the sudden change in temperature. To do this, set trays or pots in a sheltered spot outside, increasing the amount of time they're out there each day, starting with 2 to 3 hours, then increasing the time outside slowly over the course of a week or two, at which point seedlings can remain outside from then on. This helps the young plants acclimate to the more extreme temperature fluctuations found outdoors.

SUPPORTING YOUR FLOWERS

It is devastating to have a full bed of thriving, gorgeous blooms knocked over by heavy spring rains or a summer windstorm. Providing plants with some type of support is the key to growing long, straight stems and avoiding potential weather damage. These four methods are what I use most frequently to keep the plants in my cutting garden standing tall.

CORRALLING

When you have an entire bed of tall, bulky plants like chrysanthemums, cosmos, or dahlias, building a post-and-string corral around them is the fastest and easiest way to provide support. Pound in heavy wooden or metal posts that are tall enough so that 4 to 5 feet (1.2 to 1.5 m) is above ground at each of the four corners of the bed, along with additional posts placed every 8 to 10 feet (2.3 to 3 m) along the sides of the bed. Run twine 3 feet (1 m) above ground around the outside perimeter of the posts, making sure to pull it as tight as possible as you go. This will keep plants from falling over and spilling out into the paths. For plants more than 4 feet (1.2 m) tall, use a second layer of twine, spaced 1 foot (30 cm) higher.

NETTING

For airy plants that produce an abundance of branching stems—like bells of Ireland, black-eyed Susan, celosia, chrysanthemums, false Queen Anne's lace, snapdragons, and zinnias—use plastic netting with 6-inch (15-cm) squares. Immediately after planting, or before plants reach 1 foot (30 cm) tall, pound in heavy wooden or metal stakes at each corner of the bed and then around the perimeter of the bed so that they stick up about 4 feet (1.2 m) at a spacing of roughly 8 feet (2.4 m) apart. Secure the netting about 18 inches (46 cm) above ground, by either pulling it tight over the stakes or securing it to the stakes with zip ties, so that it's suspended like a sheet over the plants. As the plants gain height, they grow right up through the netting, which gives them the necessary support to stand up to both wind and rain. Large, bulky flowers like chrysanthemums require two layers of netting spaced roughly a foot (30 cm) apart.

STAKING

For large plants that are bulky and need some extra support, such as delphinium or individually planted dahlias, give each its own stake. When plants are about 1 foot (30 cm) tall, pound sturdy, 3- to 4-foot (1- to 1.2-m) tall stakes a couple of inches/cm from the plant bases. As the plants grow, loosely tie the stems to stakes with twine or string every 6 to 8 inches (15 to 20 cm).

TRELLISING

Vigorous climbers such as clematis, cup-and-saucer vine, and sweet peas grow rapidly, and it's important to have a strong framework in place before you plant them. Create a sturdy trellis using 6-foot (1.8-m) tall wooden or metal posts. Space posts 8 to 10 feet (2.4 to 3 m) apart down your row and attach 6-foot (1.8-m) tall metal fencing (such as chicken wire) to the posts using baling wire or zip ties. As the vines grow, secure them to the fencing when they're about 1 foot (30 cm) tall by running a layer of twine around the outside perimeter. This will hold them snuggly against the trellis so that they don't fall over in the wind or rain. For fast growers like sweet peas and bush nasturtiums that don't have clinging tendrils, add a new layer of twine up the fencing every week.

PINCHING

When it comes to summer flowering annuals that have a branching form, pinching is one of the most important techniques. The practice of pinching encourages plants to produce more branches near the base, which increases the total number of flowering stems per plant as well as longer stem length.

Here's how it's done: when plants are young, between 8 and 12 inches (20 and 30 cm) tall, take sharp pruners and snip the top 3 to 4 inches (7 to 10 cm) off of the plant, just above a set of leaves. This signals the plant to send up multiple stems from below where the cut was made, resulting in more abundant flower production. Amaranth, branching sunflowers, celosia (all except Bombay celosia), cosmos, dahlias, snapdragons, and zinnias all benefit greatly from being pinched.

I pinch only those annual plants that produce flowers on multiple stems. Do not use this method for varieties that produce just one flower per plant, such as single stem sunflowers and Bombay celosia. Throughout the book, I will share tips for which plants benefit from this treatment, and at what stage you should pinch, for best results.

CARING FOR CUT FLOWERS

It's a deeply thrilling experience to stroll through the cutting garden, harvesting armloads of fresh flowers that you grew yourself to create a beautiful arrangement. After so many months of hard work and careful tending, the bounty is a priceless reward.

Throughout the book, I share my tried-and-true tricks for getting the longest vase life from each individual variety. In addition to these specific tips, the following are important techniques to help you get the most from your cut flowers.

CLEAN AND SANITIZE BUCKETS AND VASES BEFORE USE

This is one of the most important things you can do to extend the vase life of your cut flowers. A good rule of thumb is that vessels should be clean enough to drink from. Dirty containers are hosts to bacteria, which will plug up stems and prevent them from taking up water, and will decrease the flowers' vase life significantly.

HARVEST FLOWERS AND FOLIAGE DURING THE COOLEST HOURS OF THE DAY

Either in the morning or evening is when plants are the most plump and hydrated and will recover most quickly from the shock of being cut.

PICK BLOOMS AT THE RIGHT STAGE OF MATURITY FOR THE LONGEST SHOW

Every variety has an ideal time to be cut, which I share in each plant profile. But for the most part, harvesting flowers before they've fully opened, and before the bees have found them, is best. Once pollinated, flowers are signaled to start making seeds, and their vase life is inherently shortened.

PLACE STEMS INTO COOL, CLEAN WATER

As you harvest, remove leaves from the lower half of the stems, and place immediately into cool, clean water. This will minimize wilting, since there is less foliage to rehydrate. The easiest way to do this is to carry a bucket with you into the garden at harvest time.

LET THE STEMS REST

Place buckets of freshly picked stems in a cool spot, out of direct sunlight, to rest for a few hours before arranging. This gives the flowers and foliage a chance to fully rehydrate.

ADD FLORAL PRESERVATIVE

This "flower food" contains three important ingredients: sugar, an acidifier, and a biocide. Mix them with your vase water, and these ingredients will keep your flowers fed, keep the water acidic enough for flowers to continue drinking, and stop harmful bacteria from forming in the vase. My favorite type, Floralife Crystal Clear, can be ordered online. Add 1 teaspoon (5 g) of the powdered preservative to each quart/liter of water and stir well before adding flowers.

RECUT STEMS

Recut stems at an angle with sharp pruners before placing flowers and foliage in the vase. This will encourage them to continue drinking steadily.

CUT STEMS: SPECIAL CASES

DIRTY FLOWERS

A few flower types are lovingly referred to in the trade as "dirty flowers." These varieties are notorious for turning water murky really fast, even with floral preservative added to the water. Black-eyed Susan, sunflowers, yarrow, and zinnias are all members of this club. To combat their messy behavior and extend their vase life, add a few drops of bleach to the water along with the floral preservative.

WIMPY DRINKERS

A number of flowers and foliage types are amazing in the vase but can sometimes be difficult to get hydrated after picking. For these treasures, dip their stem ends into boiling water, or hold the stem ends over an open flame, for 7 to 10 seconds, at which point you will notice the stems changing color and texture. Then place them in a vase of cool water. This treatment works well for basil, cerinthe, Iceland poppies, mint, and scented geranium, but can also be tried on anything that's prone to wilting. I use the boiling water method for most crops because it's easiest (I can dip an entire handful of flowers at once), but a flame is more effective for Iceland poppies.

WOODY BRANCHES

Many flowering trees and shrubs make wonderful cutting material, but getting their woody stems to take up water can be tricky. As soon as you harvest these stems, remove the lower half of their leaves and use heavy clippers to split their woody stem ends vertically a few inches up. Then place them directly into a bucket of cool, fresh water to rest until arranging.

39

Tools of the Trade

Having the right tools for the job makes tasks go faster, and if they are designed ergonomically, they can lessen the impact that the hard labor of gardening can have on your body. Over the years I've tested dozens of different tools in search of the perfect ones. The following are what I think every cut flower grower needs in their arsenal.

GARDENING TOOLS

BACKPACK SPRAYER I use a 3-gallon (11.3-L) Solo backpack sprayer for applying compost tea and fish emulsion. If you're using herbicides or pesticides in your garden, be sure to designate separate sprayers for each and label them clearly. I've seen many growers accidentally kill their entire crop because they grabbed the wrong sprayer from the shed.

BUTTER KNIFE This is the best tool for transplanting small plugs into preburned landscape fabric (see page 29) because it's lightweight, easy to use, and narrow enough to slip into the planting holes.

COLLINEAR HOE With its ergonomic design, this hoe allows you to stand straight up while cultivating. Its thin, sharp blade glides just below the soil surface, cutting off weeds at their roots. The lightweight, upright design turns the tedious task of weeding into a speedy, meditative joy.

EARTHWAY SEEDER Fast and easy to use, this walk-behind seeder opens the furrow, plants seed at preset spacing, covers the seed, and packs the soil down while marking the next row, all in one easy step. I use it for direct seeding hardy annuals in the autumn as well as fast-germinating summer crops like sunflowers and zinnias.

FARMER-FLORIST TOOL BELT Having essential tools handy is my key to efficiency. This leather tool belt (see "Resources," page 304) has room to carry two types of pruners, a cell phone, and a pen or pencil. I can take notes, document varieties, and harvest, all without running back to my office or tool shed.

FLOWER SNIPS Lightweight needle-nose flower snips are my go-to for everyday harvesting; they work well on both delicate blooms like sweet peas and thicker stems like dahlias and zinnias. They are perfectly shaped to rest in the palm of your hand, so you can harvest for hours without getting a sore wrist.

GARDEN CART I use ours for hauling just about anything, including trays of transplants, buckets of water, hand tools, and flowers.

GLOVES A pair of heavy-duty leather gloves are a must for pruning roses and cleaning out overgrown garden areas, but my daily go-to gloves are a lightweight nitrile-coated version because they are durable and breathable, and they wash easily.

HEAVY METAL RAKE This is great for spreading out compost and smoothing out beds before laying fabric or seeding.

HORI HORI KNIFE I love this knife for hand weeding, transplanting small plugs, and planting larger things like dahlia tubers and perennials.

JAPANESE HAND HOE Well balanced, lightweight, and sturdy, this sharp little gem is my all-time favorite short-handled hoe.

LONG-HANDLED PITCHFORK I use a pitchfork for pitching compost and mulch onto beds and also for turning over garden beds and digging up dahlia tubers and other bulbs in the fall.

LONG-HANDLED SHOVEL Every gardener needs a good shovel, preferably one with a nice strong handle. It has an array of uses, including turning beds, double digging, moving soil, prying out rocks, and transplanting.

LONG-HANDLED WIRE WEEDER This long-handled, ergonomically designed hoe is ideal for precision weeding while standing up.

PRUNERS A pair of heavy-duty pruners is a must-have for pruning woody stemmed plants. My favorite brand is ARS, because their blades are chrome plated to resist rust and the handles are ergonomically designed.

SMALL METAL LEAF RAKE This is one of the most versatile tools; I use it to spread fertilizer evenly on beds, mulch, and clean up debris from the top of fabric beds.

WHEEL HOE For gardeners cultivating more than half an acre, where landscape fabric isn't being used, the wheel hoe is ideal for managing weeds in aisles and in between rows. It's twice as fast as hand hoeing, and with a little practice can be incredibly precise.

WHEELBARROW The 6-cubic-foot (1.8-cubic-m) wheelbarrow belly is the perfect size for moving large amounts of compost and weeds but still small enough to be manageable. After losing some of my favorite wheelbarrows to rust, I now opt for plastic.

FLORIST'S TOOLBOX

Having the right supplies for flower arranging is the key to being able to get down to business when inspiration strikes. The following are what I keep on hand in my flower studio.

CHICKEN WIRE A great alternative to toxic flower foam, a ball of chicken wire inserted into a vase provides a sturdy framework to keep heavier stems upright.

FABRIC SCISSORS It's essential to designate a sharp pair of fabric scissors for ribbon only to preserve the blades' sharp edges. Tie a piece of ribbon to the handle as a reminder not to use them for cutting paper or wire.

FLORAL ADHESIVE CLAY I use this water-proof adhesive to secure flower frogs to the bottom of vases. It's available in green or white; I prefer the green, because it seems to be more durable and long lasting.

FLORAL STEM WRAP Adhering to itself when gently stretched, this tape is great for bouton-nieres, corsages, and flower crowns. It's available in an array of colors, but I find the light green the most versatile.

FLOWER FROGS Available in pin or cage style, flower frogs can be found at craft stores, but I also scour antique stores and flea markets to find more unique shapes and sizes. Secured with floral adhesive clay to the bottom of a vase, flower frogs allow you to use heavy, woody branches in shallow vessels without fear of their toppling out.

FLOWER SNIPS I mentioned these in the gardening tools section; they're also essential when working with bouquets.

GLOVES Lightweight nitrile gloves are my daily go-to's because they are durable, breathable, and easy to clean. They're great to have on hand when working with thorny materials like bells of Ireland and roses, and for protecting your hands from the irritating sap of false Queen Anne's lace.

PADDLE WIRE Available at most craft stores, this continuous spool of wire is ideal for making wreaths and garlands. You can also cut smaller pieces off the spool to attach little bundles of interesting materials to wreaths and garlands. And it's available in precut pieces (often labeled as floral wire) as well. I prefer the 22-gauge type of both paddle and precut floral wire.

PAPER-COVERED WIRE Available in both green and brown, this handy wire makes the perfect base for a flower crown and is what I use to attach garlands to banisters and doorways.

PRUNERS A pair of heavy-duty pruners is great to have on hand for larger woody branches and cutting through multiple stems at once. Again, I prefer the ARS brand for their ergonomically designed handles and chrome-plated blades.

ROSE STRIPPER This handy little tool makes removing thorns from roses and other prickly stems fast and easy.

RUBBER BANDS I always keep a few on hand out in the garden. Number 19 is the perfect size for bunching flowers.

TWINE Simple, natural jute works well for tying bouquets and also for making garlands.

WATER TUBES These miniature vessels hold enough water to keep a flower fresh for a day or two. Available in varying lengths, these are essential for adding flowers to premade garlands or wreaths.

WATERPROOF FLORAL TAPE This sturdy tape is perfect for securing chicken wire in a vase and wrapping bouquets for extra support. The ¼-inch (0.6-cm) size is my favorite.

WIRE WREATH FRAME Available in numerous sizes from most craft stores, these frames provide a sturdy base for wreath making.

S P R

AWAKENING TO NEW
POSSIBILITIES

Of the four seasons, spring is most certainly my favorite. The sun finally returns to our rainy part of the world, and new growth can be spotted around every corner. Mornings at our farm are filled with bird songs and the smell of warm earth, while the scents of freshly cut grass and flowering trees hang in the air until dusk. With so much promise and possibility, I find myself walking around with a perpetual smile.

Spring brings with it a busy hum of activity. We sow tens of thousands of seeds in our warm greenhouse and nestle hundreds of baby plants into the ground. Once the first flowers arrive and need to be harvested, life can get a little chaotic. I spend my days weeding, preparing beds, planting, harvesting, and bunching flowers from dawn until dusk.

This is the time of the year when I'm most prone to overdo it, both by working too long in the garden and by planting too many seeds. I find it nearly impossible to remember that each tiny seed will eventually grow into a magnificent plant that requires space, attention, tending, and harvesting. It is so tempting to grow a ton of extra seedlings. I constantly have to rein myself in and stick to the master plan I created.

Spring
Tasks

PLANT SEEDS

Quite possibly my all-time favorite flower-growing task is starting seeds in the greenhouse in spring; we start about 75 percent of our cutting garden in the 3 months of this season. Tearing open each little packet, then tucking the tiny seeds into soil-filled pots just never gets old, no matter how many times I do it. I sow hardy annuals that can handle colder temps and bloom early—such as larkspur, love-in-a-mist, and false Queen Anne's lace—as soon as the spring equinox arrives, followed by a second and third sowing of the same plants a few weeks later. Heat lovers such as basil, celosia, marigolds, and zinnias are all started later, about 2 to 3 weeks before the last spring frost.

DIVIDE DAHLIAS

A few weeks before our last spring frost, I pull boxes of dahlia tubers from their winter storage spot in the basement and assess them for any damage. I go through each clump individually and toss any rotten, moldy, or shriveled tubers and then start the process of dividing. (See page 135 for detailed instructions on dividing.) To get a jump on the season, you can divide tubers in earliest spring, plant in pots, and set them in a warm greenhouse to bring them into growth ahead of schedule. Then, once the last spring frost has passed, plant the already leafed-out dahlias in the garden for flowers that'll appear up to 6 weeks sooner than those planted from tubers in the ground at the same time.

PREPARE THE SOIL

One of the biggest undertakings in spring is getting the ground ready for planting. Spending a little extra time on this step, and really doing it right, will pay off throughout the rest of the year with an abundance of blooms and foliage. In the "Basics" chapter, I detailed how to take a soil test and feed your soil. I generally begin this in early spring, about a month before planting in the ground, to ensure I have enough time to get it done, and also to allow the compost and other amendments time to settle into the soil.

53

PLANT SEEDLINGS

On warm spring days, you may be fooled into thinking that it's safe to plant tender seedlings outside. But pay close attention to your last spring frost date—you can ask your local nursery if you're unsure of the date—and the cold hardiness of your plants, since some can't handle the low temperatures that can surprise us this time of year. Hardy annuals like cerinthe, larkspur, love-in-a-mist, false Queen Anne's lace, and snapdragons can be set out when nights are still chilly and tolerate some light frosts unscathed. I generally start tucking these into the garden up to a month before our last frost date, and if below-freezing weather threatens, I cover them with a layer or two of frost cloth until the cold spell passes.

But warm weather lovers that bloom in summer and fall—like celosia, dahlias, marigolds, and zinnias—are not nearly as hardy, and will die if they get too cold. These types of flowers should be planted outside only after all threat of frost has passed and the soil temperature has reached 50°F (10°C). In my area, this is usually 2 to 3 weeks after our last spring frost. Keep in mind that all young plants need to be steadily nurtured for the first month after they've been set out into the garden, to ensure healthy, strong growth. Water deeply right after planting, and continue to irrigate often enough to keep the ground moist but not soggy—for me, this is once a week—through the remainder of the growing year.

WEED

As the days lengthen and the sun starts to warm the soil, weeds appear en masse almost overnight—and managing them is one of the most important tasks in spring. In order for your plants to have the best chance at a healthy life, it is essential to keep their growing area as weed-free as possible. The best, and easiest, time to weed is as soon as you see the tiny seedlings emerge. Using a thin collinear hoe, run the blade an inch (2.5 cm) below the soil's surface, slicing off the young weeds at their roots. This should be done weekly to stay ahead of the rampant growth. Weeding by hand works well, too; just be sure to do it regularly and while weeds are still young.

54

MULCH

One of the easiest ways to prevent weeds and retain soil moisture is by mulching around the base of plants. There are many materials that work; the key is to get mulch in place before weeds emerge. At my farm, we use landscape fabric for both walking paths and growing beds, since our soil is loaded with weed seeds; we find this the most effective way to cover a large area. (Find detailed instructions for using landscape fabric on page 28.)

For large permanent plants like trees and shrubs, wood chips make amazing mulch. Early in the season, I place a layer of cardboard around the base of these plants—making sure the edges overlap so no ground is exposed—then wet it with water so that it forms to the soil, and heap 4 to 5 inches (10 to 13 cm) of wood chips or wood shavings on top. (Be sure to keep mulch from directly touching the plant's trunk or base, since this can cause rot, and don't use cedar chips, as they will inhibit the plants' growth.) I apply a fresh layer of wood chips each spring, and it keeps the weeds at bay for an entire year!

For smaller plants like dahlias, perennials, and most annuals, I find that aged compost, dried grass clippings, aged leaves, and straw all work well. Don't use hay; it contains a lot of weed seeds that will only worsen your problem.

STAKE PLANTS

In the spring, the garden quickly goes from nearly bare dirt to a sea of green and then to a rainbow of bloom. Nearly all cutting garden plants put on such rapid growth that it's necessary to stake them early on.

Netting and staking both perennials and annuals is essential for getting long straight stems and not losing big swaths of your floral bounty to heavy spring rains that will topple lush growth. There are numerous staking options, including bamboo canes, metal plant cages, welded wire, and plastic netting with 6-inch (15-cm) squares for plants that most need support. I mention what works best in the plant profiles that follow. The key is to get the staking in place while the plants are still young so that they grow through or around the supports and you don't damage them by trying to stake when they're already mature.

56

Spring
Bloomers

BIENNIALS

Biennials are a unique group of plants that produce only leaves the first year, and in the second year they flower, set seed, and die. What makes them such treasures is that they fill the wide gap between the last of the tulips and the first of the hardy annuals in the garden. Also, the more you pick these blooms, the more they flower. They are real spring garden workhorses.

HOW TO GROW

Start seeds later than most, at the end of spring, and plant seedlings in the garden at the end of summer. Ideally, plants will have at least 6 weeks to establish before the first autumn frost. Once planted, each variety will produce a large clump of foliage before cold weather sets in and then sit dormant through the autumn and winter, reawakening to bloom during the later months of spring. Seed and plants for all of the varieties are easy to grow and generally hardy down to 30°F (−1°C).

FAVORITE VARIETIES

CANTERBURY BELLS (*Campanula medium*) It is easy to see why this old cottage garden favorite is still a must-have for any cut flower grower. Both the single and the double varieties produce huge stems loaded with balloon-shaped blooms—in colors including white, pink, lavender, and purple—that are unique and long lasting in the vase. The plants are quite bulky, so stake them with netting at planting time to keep them upright in heavy spring rains. **Vase life tricks:** Pick when the top bud is colored and just opening. It is not unheard of to have these stems last 2 weeks in a bouquet.

COLUMBINE Although these are perennials, I have found that treating them as biennials, and replanting fresh stock each season, means a much greater harvest each spring. Older plants seem to succumb to disease after a year or two, and their self-sown babies aren't numerous enough for a meaningful crop. There are many, many varieties to choose from, and almost all are good for cutting. The Barlow Series is a lovely group of tall, double-flowered plants that often produce 7 to 10 stems each if grown in rich soil. Another phenomenal series, called Tower, has massive 3½-foot (106-cm) stems topped with dozens of large, fully double blooms that resemble upturned petticoats. While the bloom window is short, these beauties are definitely worth the garden space. **Vase life tricks:** Cut the flowers early in development (before any begin to drop their petals) for the longest vase life.

FOXGLOVE There is so much to love about this beautiful and graceful flower. When I was a little girl it was scattered throughout our garden, and I loved watching hungry bees nestle inside the freckled blooms to gather pollen. There are many varieties to choose from, but my all-time favorites are 'Alba' and 'Apricot Beauty'. **Vase life tricks:** I've found that once the blooms are pollinated, they drop from the stems, so be sure to harvest early, when just a few bottom blossoms are open, for the longest vase life.

MONEY PLANT (*Lunaria annua*) Grown primarily for its beautiful seedpods, this spring treasure thrives in less-than-ideal conditions, including shade and poor soil. (Flowers can be harvested in early spring, but the window of bloom is so short that it isn't a very reliable flower crop.) I love to use the seedpods when they're green; as they age a little on the plant, they take on a purple cast. Each plant produces 20 to 30 long stems that are loaded with brilliant green seed cases. They can also be dried for later use in autumn wreaths and bouquets. To dry, hang freshly cut stems upside

59

MONEY PLANT

SWEET WILLIAM

down in a warm, dark place for 2 to 3 weeks or until they are firm to the touch. Be gentle when handling them after they've dried, because the seedpods are fragile and can fall apart easily. **Vase life tricks:** The pods last for well over a week when fresh, and need no special treatment.

SWEET ROCKET (*Hesperis matronalis*) This cottage garden favorite comes in white, violet, or a mix, which occasionally includes a pretty mauve pink. Easy to grow, it is one of the first flowers in the garden not grown from a bulb. Blooms are highly scented and look fantastic in bouquets. The more you harvest, the more they flower. After blooms fade, the stems are loaded with pretty seedpods resembling thin, shiny green beans. I like to mix them into bouquets as well. Note that stems do lengthen a bit in water after harvest, like tulips, so if you're incorporating these into bouquets, snug them down a little lower than seems

right in the beginning to allow for elongation. **Vase life tricks:** It'll look good for a week or more, and needs no special care.

SWEET WILLIAM Of all the biennials I grow, these sturdy plants are the most productive in the spring garden. While they aren't a huge show-stopper when it comes to looks, they add nice color and fragrance to mixed bouquets and have an extremely long vase life. They are also easy to grow, hardy, and usually quite healthy even with minimal care. I love the Tall Double Mix and two dark foliage varieties, 'Oeschberg' and 'Sooty'. **Vase life tricks:** Harvest when just a few flowers are open on a head. This prevents the blossoms in the garden from getting damaged by rain, and will give the stems a 2-week vase life.

FOXGLOVE

SWEET ROCKET

COLUMBINE

CANTERBURY BELLS

DAFFODILS

I used to think there was only one kind of daffodil—the big, garishly bright, cheap ones that are sold at every grocery store in spring. But when I visited a seventh-generation Dutch flower grower's field a few springs ago, I was introduced to an entirely new world of specialty daffodils that I hadn't even known existed, and I've been hooked on their beauty and charm ever since.

Daffodils are a diverse group with great appeal—you can find varieties that are miniature, fragrant, ruffled, double bloomed, and multicolored. They are hardy, easy to grow, and rarely plagued by pests or disease. They also multiply rapidly, which means that if you make a small initial investment in bulbs, you'll be rewarded with more and more blooms in the years to come. But the best thing about growing these delightful flowers is that they arrive in early spring, long before the rest of the garden wakes up.

HOW TO GROW

For the best selection of varieties, order bulbs in late summer and plant them as soon as they arrive in autumn. No special treatment is needed other than amending the soil with compost (as detailed on page 27) and adding some bulb fertilizer in the planting hole. The rule of thumb when planting daffodils is to place bulbs at a depth two times the bulb's height, and as far apart as they are wide.

To grow as cut flowers, plant daffodils in long, straight rows. In addition to growing them in your cutting beds, you can scatter them into your mixed garden beds and borders, and harvest from wherever they're growing. After the flowers have faded and the foliage starts to look unattractive, it is important to resist the urge to cut them back; hold off until the leaves have turned yellow and start to fall over. This is a sign that the photosynthesis process (which nourishes the bulbs for the following year) is over and it's safe to prune them to the ground.

Daffodils multiply rapidly, and in just 2 or 3 years after planting, you'll have at least double what you started with. The ideal time to dig and divide bulbs is when the leaves have started to fade and turn yellow in early summer. Using a pitchfork or spade, dig under the cluster of bulbs and gently separate them, then replant. Divide bulbs at least once every 4 years.

FAVORITE VARIETIES

Of the 22 daffodil varieties that are planted on my farm, the following are my all-time favorites.

'FLOWER DRIFT' This beautiful single-flowered variety has the most cheerful ivory and orange petals that overlap and fold together in an unforgettable display.

'ORANGERY' The unique, white-and-yellow frilled petals of this split type are especially eye-catching.

'PETIT FOUR' Of all the daffodils I have seen and grown, none quite compares to the beauty and elegance of this particular variety. Its ivory-pointed outer petals perfectly frame the doublecrown, which is filled with an exquisite mix of apricot pink, buttercream, and peach frilled petals. If I could grow only one daffodil, this surely would be it.

'PINK CHARM' This is a stunning variety with ivory petals and a delicate peachy-pink throat. The loveliest of the pink types we grow, these flowers look as if they were stolen from a 16th-century Dutch painting. They are romantic, classic, unique, and beautiful.

'PETIT FOUR'

'FLOWER DRIFT'

'PINK CHARM'

'SIR WINSTON CHURCHILL'

'TAHITI'

'YELLOW CHEERFULNESS'

'ORANGERY'

'SIR WINSTON CHURCHILL' This variety has thick stems topped with dense white, multi-headed blooms that have a strong fragrance.

'TAHITI' The vibrant, ruffly yellow petals alternate with red ones in the center. Its tall, strong stems and large blooms make it a great cut flower.

'YELLOW CHEERFULNESS' One of the last varieties to bloom in the garden, this small-flowered beauty is a must-grow. It is highly fragrant and lasts up to a week in the vase.

VASE LIFE TRICKS

Generally, all daffodil varieties have a vase life of nearly a week if harvested before the flowers are fully open. Keep in mind that when cut, daffodils ooze a slimy sap that is toxic to other flowers and will shorten their vase life significantly. To avoid affecting other blooms in an arrangement, you'll need to "condition" the daffodils first. To do this, place freshly cut stems into cool water, on their own, for 2 to 3 hours; during that time, the stem ends will callus over and the toxic sap will stop flowing. After that, don't recut the daffodil stems when adding to arrangements, because the sap will start leaking all over again. Of course, you can create an arrangement solely of daffodils, either just one variety or several, and the sap won't be an issue.

DELICATE-FLOWERED BULBS

During the early months of spring, plenty of new growth sprouts from trees and shrubs, but many flowers have yet to appear. This is when bulbs come in to save the day. One of the most dramatic plant groups, bulbs are the backbone of any spring cutting garden. Their showy blooms, vibrant colors, soft scents, and miniature details make them truly irresistible.

While well-known types such as tulips and daffodils bring a lot to the party, the lesser-known treasures that follow can increase your early spring bounty. Filling your cutting garden with a wide variety of blooming bulbs means that you'll have an abundant stream of flower ingredients to pick from for months.

HOW TO GROW

Bulbs require very little attention or care to thrive, so they are perfect for beginning cut flower gardeners. As long as you plant them on time, in fertile soil and full sun, you'll be rewarded come spring.

Because most bulbs require some winter chilling to flower properly, they need to be planted in autumn. For mild winter regions, look into buying prechilled bulbs.

Before planting, prepare the soil following the directions outlined in "Digging In" (page 27). As a rule of thumb, plant bulbs twice as deep as they are tall, and the same distance apart as they are wide, in a row. Once tucked into the soil, bulbs will form roots all winter long. Then, in early spring, they will push through the soil into a glorious flower display.

FAVORITE VARIETIES

ANEMONE Unlike the other varieties listed here, which produce only 1 or 2 blooms per bulb, anemones flower abundantly for many months, often making 20 to 25 flowers over the course of spring. Be sure to cut spent flowers down to the base to promote new blooms. More tender than other bulbs, anemones require some extra winter protection. We plant them in low tunnels in the autumn, and when extremely cold weather (below 25°F/–4°C) strikes, I add an additional layer of frost cloth over the plants themselves, under the tunnels for extra insulation. The corms (which are similar to bulbs) resemble little brown acorns. When you get them in autumn, soak them for 24 hours before planting. Then poke them into the soil 2 inches (5 cm), pointy end down. After a few weeks, small green shoots will push up from the soil, and a canopy of green will persist through winter until they send up buds in early spring. **Vase life tricks:** Extremely long lasting, anemones easily persist for 10 days in the vase if harvested as soon as they open. Adding flower food to the water will ensure that the flowers stay brilliantly colored.

FRITILLARIA These unique bell-shaped flowers are breathtaking in full bloom. A relative newcomer to my garden, these stunning bulbs are quickly climbing to the top of my favorites list. I've grown numerous varieties, but the towering, plum-black blooms of *Fritillaria persica* are the most amazing of all—each 3-foot (1-m) stem is loaded with dozens of inky purple, upside-down bells. **Vase life tricks:** Harvest when half to three-quarters of the blossoms are open and place in water mixed with floral preservative. They should last a week in the vase.

68

FRITILLARIA

GRAPE HYACINTH

LEUCOJUM

ANEMONE

HYACINTH

GRAPE HYACINTH (*Muscari azureum*) These adorable miniature treasures feel like the biggest luxury when picking for a bouquet. To harvest, tug the stems at the bottom quickly upward and they'll pop off the base easily, giving you long stems. Two of my favorite varieties are 'Ocean Magic' and 'Valerie Finnis'. **Vase life tricks:** Pick when a third of the florets are open and place in water with flower preservative for a week of vase life.

HYACINTH By far the most fragrant spring flower I've ever grown, these heady blooms are available in a wide range of colors, including soft yellow, apricot, sky blue, deep purple, lavender, white, magenta, and azure. They're beautiful displayed alone or mixed with other flowers in arrangements. **Vase life tricks:** If picked when just a third to half of the blossoms are open, these stems will last for 7 to 10 days in the vase.

LEUCOJUM 'GRAVETYE GIANT' If fairies existed, these blooms would certainly become their hats. Each 12- to 18-inch (30- to 45-cm) stem bears a collection of delicate white bells, sporting a tiny green dot at the tip of each petal. **Vase life tricks:** Harvest when two-thirds of the flowers have unfurled and place in water mixed with preservative for a vase life of 7 to 10 days. These blooms leak a clear sap, so condition them by placing in cool water for a few hours before mixing with other stems.

FLOWERING
BRANCHES

Each spring, as the trees begin their flamboyant display, I make it a point to stop and stand under as many as I possibly can. To me, there is nothing more magical than standing under the canopy of a tree in full bloom. Flowering shrubs are equally mesmerizing, with their bloom-laden stems arching under the weight of the flower show. Staring into blossom-filled branches and soaking in their beauty is one of spring's most indulgent treats.

When we moved to our little farm, the property already contained a few large, mature trees and shrubs that have provided the backbone of all of my early spring bouquets. Over time, I've made it a point to plant at least one or two rows of new additions each year. It's taken some time for them all to mature, but I now have a few hundred trees and bushes to clip from. Since they serve a dual purpose—both as blooms early in the year, and as foliage and fruiting stems from summer through autumn—I harvest from them way more than I expected. So, if you have the space, my advice is to plant more flowering trees and shrubs than you think you'll use.

HOW TO GROW

The following deciduous trees and shrubs are easy to grow, and they thrive in most climates. Choose a spot with well-draining soil in full sunlight, making sure to give the plants plenty of room to stretch out as they grow. I made the mistake of planting many of mine too close together, and over time I have had to transplant them because they crowded each other out. The best time to plant trees and shrubs is during the autumn if you're starting with potted plants, or winter if you're starting with bare roots.

FAVORITE VARIETIES

Once you start learning about deciduous trees and shrubs with spring-flowering branches, you'll discover just how many choices you have. I've grown a little of everything over the years; the following are the easiest to cultivate and most abundantly producing of all.

DOUBLEFILE VIBURNUM (*Viburnum plicatum tomentosum*) This is one of my all-time favorite shrubs. It flowers magnificently in spring, and as the blossoms fade, it leaves behind an abundance of rich green, architectural branches that are a great base for bouquets. It gets quite tall, often reaching 8 to 10 feet (2.4 to 3 m), so give the plant a spot where it can really spread out.

FLOWERING CHERRY Nothing can compare to a fully mature cherry, with its spreading, blossom-laden stems swaying in the breeze—it's one of the most magnificent blooming trees there is. There are numerous varieties to choose from, but my favorite is 'Kanzan', a double-flowered pink beauty that blooms later than most.

FLOWERING CRABAPPLE Years ago I discovered the magic of crabapple trees and have since planted over a dozen on my little farm. Of all the varieties I've grown and worked with, the French cultivar (meaning a cultivated variety) 'Evereste' always steals the show. The fat pink buds give way to double creamy blooms that carry a light, citrusy fragrance. In addition to being a beautiful spring bloomer, the trees are disease free and produce a bumper crop of marble-sized miniature apples that look smashing in bouquets from midsummer through late autumn.

FLOWERING CHERRY

HAWTHORN This beautiful tree flowers for a few glorious weeks each spring, then produces an abundance of small, deep-red fruits that cover its craggy branches in the autumn. Depending on the variety, flowers can be pink, white, or red. Be careful when handling these, because the stems have wicked thorns. Cut branches when flowers are still in bud or just opening.

SNOWBALL BUSH (*Viburnum opulus*) The towering branches smothered in fluffy, creamy round flowers really do make this bush look like a pile of snowballs. Its vigorous growth habit, carefree nature, and abundant blooming make it a real winner.

VASE LIFE TRICKS

Because these flowers are on woody branches, they require a little extra effort to get them to last in the vase. If you follow these tricks, cut stems will last for up to a week in water. Harvest when it's cool in the morning or evening, and immediately strip the bottom third of the stems of their foliage. Then, using clippers, split the woody stem ends vertically for a few inches (cm) and place them directly into a bucket of cool, fresh water. Let them rest for a few hours before arranging. Using flower food in the water will help prolong the life of cut branches.

HAWTHORN

DOUBLEFILE VIBURNUM

FLOWERING CRABAPPLE

SNOWBALL BUSH

HARDY
ANNUALS

Hardy annuals are some of the hardest working, most productive plants in the late spring/early summer cutting garden. Their ability to withstand cold temperatures, thrive with minimal care, and produce abundantly for more than a month from just one sowing makes them an indispensable addition to the cut flower garden.

HOW TO GROW

In cold climates, start seeds of these plants indoors or in a greenhouse in early spring. After seedlings have 3 sets of true leaves, plant them outdoors while the weather is still cool, usually about a month before the last spring frost. They are quite tough and can handle some chill, so they need no major protection during periods of frost. In milder climates, plant them in the garden in autumn for an even earlier spring bloom.

All of these plants are moderately productive, and the more you pick, the more they flower. But to extend the harvest window, I highly recommend succession planting (see page 24) at least a few times for each type. I generally sow a large batch in the autumn, then another in early spring, followed by two more sowings spaced a few weeks apart after that. This approach gives me an abundance of foliage and filler for almost 3 months. Every climate is different, so you'll want to experiment a little and find which hardy annuals perform best for you, but I can guarantee these plants will become some of your favorites.

FAVORITE VARIETIES

BELLS OF IRELAND This is one of the finest annual foliage plants you can grow. It's a little tricky to start seeds, since the plants are slow to emerge; it helps to freeze the seeds for 7 to 10 days before sowing. Once sprouted, the plants grow very rapidly, so space them 18 inches (46 cm) apart. It's essential to stake this variety with flower netting (see page 36), since without support, one big rainstorm will flatten an entire patch in a matter of minutes. **Vase life tricks:** Harvest blooms once the green bells start to form along the stem. Stems will last extremely long in the vase, up to 2 weeks.

FALSE QUEEN ANNE'S LACE (*Ammi majus*) This is one of the most useful and productive filler plants that you can grow from seed. I plant hundreds of them every year and always use every single stem. The lacy flower heads and crisp green-white color provide an invaluable backbone for late spring/early summer bouquets. Plants get large, so space them 18 inches (46 cm) apart and be sure to stake them early so that they don't topple over in heavy spring rains. For staking, I recommend using flower netting attached to sturdy posts, since these plants are quite bulky. **Vase life tricks:** Sap can be irritating so I recommend wearing gloves and long sleeves when harvesting. Pick when about 80 percent of the flowers on a stem are open. If harvested much earlier, the stems have a tendency to wilt. Fresh flowers will last for 6 to 8 days in the vase with the help of flower preservative.

LOVE-IN-A-MIST

ORACH

BELLS OF IRELAND

LARKSPUR   FALSE QUEEN ANNE'S LACE   HONEYWORT

HONEYWORT (*Cerinthe major*) One of the most unusually colored flowers that I grow, a single stem of honeywort in full bloom can be silver, blue, purple, and green all at the same time. Plants are easy to grow and produce a bumper crop for many weeks. To extend the harvest, sow a new batch of seeds every 3 weeks from early spring through early summer. **Vase life tricks:** Be sure to harvest during the cool of the day and then treat stems right away by dipping the bottom into 2 to 3 inches (5 to 7 cm) of boiling water for 7 to 10 seconds and then placing them in cool water with flower preservative. Stems get very floppy immediately after harvest, but once hydrated, honeywort will straighten back up and has a long vase life of 7 to 10 days.

LARKSPUR This is easy to grow, the flowers come in a rainbow of colors, and blooms can even be dried for later use. Larkspur plants do best when sown directly in the garden (versus started in seed trays indoors). Because it is extremely cold-tolerant, larkspur can be planted in autumn in even very cold climates. For a continued harvest, sow seed in the autumn and then again every 3 to 4 weeks starting as early as the soil can be worked, up until the last spring frost date. Seed can be tricky to germinate, so pop seeds into the freezer for a week before planting; then they will sprout readily. **Vase life tricks:** Harvest larkspur when a third of the blossoms are open on a stem for the longest vase life. If you use floral preservative, you can expect larkspur to last in the vase for a solid week. To dry, let all but the top 3 or 4 blooms open, then pick and hang upside down in a warm, dry place out of bright light for 2 weeks.

LOVE-IN-A-MIST (*Nigella*) While this plant looks quite fragile, it is actually one of the hardiest early bloomers around. In addition to producing unique lacy, star-shaped flowers in a mix of blues, plums, and whites, they also make football-shaped seedpods in green, chocolate, and even stripes after the flowers have faded, making them a truly hardworking cutting garden addition. The plants dislike being transplanted, so sow seeds directly in the garden. **Vase life tricks:** Harvest flowers when fully open, but before the petals have separated from the center, or else they will wilt. Vase life is generally a week, especially if you add preservative to the water. You can use the pods fresh or dried in bouquets; dried ones last almost indefinitely. To dry, harvest pods after all of the petals have fallen off, and hang the freshly cut stems upside down in a warm, dark place for 2 to 3 weeks or until they are firm to the touch. Be gentle when handling them after they've dried, because the pods can fall apart easily.

ORACH (*Atriplex*) I discovered this fantastic plant in a friend's veggie patch some years back and have been a huge fan ever since. Early in the season, the leafy stems can be harvested en masse for use as a foliage base in bouquets. If plants are left to grow, they will reward you by midsummer with gorgeous textural seed-covered stems that are also wonderful in bouquets. **Vase life tricks:** Fresh stems used for their foliage last longest when you dip the cut ends for 10 to 15 seconds in boiling water directly after harvest; seeded stems do not need any special postharvest treatment. Both can last up to 2 weeks in the vase.

ICELAND POPPIES

Not to be confused with opium poppies, Iceland poppies (*Papaver nudicale*) are one of the most exquisite cut flowers I've ever grown. Their tissue paper–like blooms and brilliantly colored petals are an alluring addition to mixed arrangements. Their beauty combined with their citrusy scent and abundant flowering habit, stretching from early spring through midsummer, make them a highly prized cutting garden addition.

Iceland poppies are technically hardy perennials and can survive even the coldest winters, but because they don't do well in high heat, they are usually grown as an annual or biennial.

HOW TO GROW

In my garden, I tuck a large batch of young plants into the ground about a month before our first autumn frost, then plant another wave of babies the following spring. This allows me to harvest, uninterrupted, from early spring through late summer.

Growing this particular flower from seed takes extra care, as they can be slow to start. In late winter, I sow just a few seeds per cell in small, soil-filled seed trays and carefully monitor them until they sprout.

Iceland poppy seeds are tiny; they look more like dust than actual seed. In fact, they're so miniscule that you need to cover them with only a very fine dusting of vermiculite or sand after sowing. For the first few weeks, bottom water (aiming to keep the soil as moist as a wrung-out sponge) by setting your seed tray in about ⅓ inch (1 cm) of standing water and letting it wick up the moisture from below so you don't accidentally wash away the babies with a powerful overhead spray. After leaves develop, water so that soil doesn't dry out, about every other day, using a gentle sprinkle from a watering can. Seed flats should be kept on heat mats that are 70°F (21°C) until seedlings emerge and develop at least 2 sets of true leaves (see the seed starting section on page 31 for details on true leaves). They can then be moved off the heat mats and grown in a warm, bright space for another 2 months until they are at least 1 inch (2.5 cm) tall, then set out into the garden.

Slugs and snails love poppies. If they're a problem where you live, after planting poppies outside, immediately apply slug bait and reapply as needed through the growing season. (I like a widely available product called Sluggo, which is safe for pets, kids, and you.) Monitor your poppies regularly for damage.

Newly transplanted poppies will begin to bloom just 6 weeks after they go into the ground, so the sooner you plant, the sooner you'll have flowers to harvest. Once flowers start blooming, it can be a full-time job to keep these beauties picked. I comb through the patch daily to snag them at just the right time. The best stage to harvest poppies is when the buds look like they're barely starting to break open. Once the flowers open fully, they're much more prone to damage by weather and rough handling.

ABOVE: COLOBRI; OPPOSITE, TOP RIGHT: CHAMPAGNE BUBBLES

FAVORITE VARIETIES

I've grown dozens of Iceland poppy varieties over the years, and so far the Champagne Bubbles Series has far outperformed the rest. This series is available in five individual colors—white, orange, pink, yellow, and scarlet—as well as a mix. I also love the Colobri line, which has really large flower heads and mixed shades. The seed is primed, so it germinates much more easily than most other varieties. The stems are thick and sturdy, and the colors are cheerful and vibrant.

VASE LIFE TRICKS

To ensure the longest vase life, use an open flame or boiling water to sear the stem ends for 7 to 10 seconds. Do this immediately after harvest, and put the treated stems into fresh water. You can then expect a solid week of bloom time.

LILACS

Lilacs are a sentimental flower for our family. My mom and Aunt Terri used to tell us how, from the time they could sit behind the wheel of their dad's pickup truck, each spring they'd go lilac stealing. In the country town of their childhood, lilacs grew in every yard, cemetery, and church garden. After dark, the sisters would drive slowly through their neighborhood alleys, one at the wheel and one in the back of the truck with loppers, secretly snipping. By the end of the run, the entire truck bed would be loaded with the stolen blooms. I can still hear their giggling voices, recounting tales of angry dogs and startled neighbors, and how they'd secretly fill their own mother's house with the flowers in the night. At the end of the story, they would always lower their voices into a serious whisper and share, "Stolen lilacs always smell the best!"

While lilacs flower for only a few short weeks each spring, their billowy blooms are an enduring favorite among flower lovers. They're easy to grow, drought tolerant, and, depending on the cultivar selected, can be hardy down to –40°F (–40°C). Some don't do well in mild-winter regions, though, so gardeners in those areas should opt for low-chill varieties (meaning the plants don't need a period of cold temperature to bloom). In some areas, lilacs grow freely in the spring—around old houses, in cemeteries, along highways, and in backyards.

HOW TO GROW

Plant lilacs in autumn, and apply a thick layer of mulch after planting to keep weeds down and to help the soil retain moisture when the weather is dry. Lilacs are slow to establish, often taking 3 to 4 years to come into flower. But I promise the wait is worth it, because once you have a happy lilac bush, it can live for decades and reward you with armloads of richly scented stems every spring.

Because lilacs are such a fleeting crop, harvest as many as you can while you have the chance. Unlike other woody shrubs, lilacs set next year's flower buds during the summer, so do any needed pruning or shaping right after bloom to avoid affecting next year's flower production. Cut long stems (thereby taking off more of the plant) when harvesting to ensure that next season's blooms will have longer, straighter stems.

FAVORITE VARIETIES

While there are many species in the lilac family, the French cultivars (*Syringa vulgaris*, also known as common lilacs) come in a wide range of colors, are extremely fragrant, and may be single or double blossomed. For gardeners in colder climates, this group is ideal because it can tolerate late freezes.

'DECLARATION' Large, fragrant clusters of reddish purple blooms smother this productive shrub every spring.

'KATHERINE HAVEMEYER' This beautiful double pink-blossomed variety looks and smells amazing in the vase.

'KRASAVITSA MOSKVY' Pale, rose-pink buds open to double pure white florets.

'MADAME FLORENT STEPMAN' Very popular in Holland, this single white-flowered variety has a delicate fragrance.

'MICHEL BUCHNER' This double, blue-lavender lilac variety has good disease resistance.

'YANKEE DOODLE' A dark purple variety, this is loaded with large panicles of single-flowered blooms.

VASE LIFE TRICKS

Cut lilacs are notoriously difficult to hydrate, and over the years I've tried every trick in the book to keep their flower heads from wilting. The following process has proven to be the most effective and will grant you the longest vase life:

- Pick flowers in the cool of morning or evening. Before you begin harvesting, fill a few large buckets about three-quarters full with fresh cool water.

- Lilacs open very little after harvest, so choose stems that have half to three-quarters of the flowers on the bloom cluster open. Note that if the blooms are fully open, their vase life will be a few days shorter.

- Immediately after harvest, transfer the blooms to a cool space. Remove many or all of the leaves so that the plant isn't putting its effort into keeping the leaves hydrated as well.

- Using heavy clippers, recut the stem ends and slice vertically up the stem 2 to 3 inches (5 to 8 cm). Then grasp one side of the sliced stem and twist backward. Plunge the freshly cut stems immediately into the cool water.

- Leave the flowers in a cool, dimly lit room for a couple of hours to rehydrate. Once fully hydrated, the lilacs can be used for arranging.

'DECLARATION'

'MADAME FLORENT
STEPMAN'

'MICHEL BUCHNER'

'KRASAVITSA
MOSKVY'

'KATHERINE
HAVEMEYER'

'YANKEE DOODLE'

PEONIES

Few flowers can contend with the ultimate queen of spring, the peony. Their large flower heads and billowy, ruffled blooms come in a dizzying array of pinks, corals, cranberries, whites, yellows, and reds. Many carry a sweet fragrance, and most are long lasting in the vase. It's no wonder they're our most requested flowers for weddings and special events.

In addition to being hugely popular and excelling in the vase, peonies are very easy to grow. They are separated into two different groups: herbaceous and tree peonies. The first group is the most commonly grown in gardens. Plants are easy to obtain, thrive in nearly every climate, and can live for over 100 years if cared for properly. Foliage emerges in early spring, and flowers are borne on the new season's growth. In late autumn, the foliage dies back to the ground. It's best to wait 2 to 3 years before harvesting from a newly planted peony; otherwise, you may affect its future growth. It's difficult to resist the urge to pick flowers during this time, but the payoff will be a fully mature plant that will reward you with years of blooms.

HOW TO GROW

Once established, peonies will flower abundantly for many years. Potted specimens can be purchased and planted in the spring, but the best results will come from bare-root stock that is dug and shipped dormant in the fall. These roots should be planted immediately so that they can start to establish before the cold of winter sets in.

Peonies prefer full sun, and you should give them at least 6 hours of uninterrupted bright daylight. Most soil types are fine, but standing water can be problematic, so be sure to find a spot that has good drainage.

Dig a hole two to three times as wide as the root, and amend the soil with a generous dose of well-rotted manure or compost and a phosphate-rich fertilizer such as bonemeal. Pay special attention to planting depth—if roots are planted too deeply they won't flower properly, so nestle the roots just below the soil surface. These plants will grow large over time, so space them at least 3 feet (1 m) apart.

In the spring, before the foliage has emerged, top-dress the soil with a sprinkle of bonemeal and a light mulch of compost, 2 inches (5 cm) deep. This will feed the new growth during the coming season.

Double-flowered types need extra staking to keep their flower heads supported under the weight of the massive blooms. Heavy spring rains can flatten a patch in a matter of minutes, so be sure to provide support early on.

If needed, in autumn, divide any mature plants that have become crowded or aren't producing well (this will happen after 8 to 10 years). Once the foliage has died to the ground, take a pitchfork, loosen the soil around the plants, and lift them out. Gently wash the roots clean of dirt so that their eyes (small, swollen red buds that will become next year's flowering stems) are visible, then split the roots apart with a sharp knife. Make sure each root has at least 3 eyes attached, and replant elsewhere in the garden.

The most problematic disease for peonies is called botrytis, and it's most common during wet spring weather. Proper plant spacing and good airflow will help, but sanitation is the real key to prevention. Monitor plants during the spring for signs of disease (including blackened, burned-looking leaves) and remove any infected foliage. Botrytis spreads rapidly, so be sure to toss the infected leaves in the garbage, not the compost. In the autumn, remove all dead foliage and instead of composting it, throw it in the trash or onto the burn pile.

'DUCHESSE DE NEMOURS'

FAVORITE VARIETIES

Peonies come in a beautiful rainbow of pastel colors, and their flower forms vary from huge crinkled doubles to fringed singles, and everything in between.

'BOWL OF BEAUTY' This is a unique variety with rose-pink outer petals surrounding a fluffy, cream-colored center.

'CORAL CHARM' One of the first to flower, this vigorous, large-headed variety comes in a warm peachy-coral blend that fades as it opens. Because of its size, stake plants early. This is one of the most popular varieties on the farm.

'DUCHESSE DE NEMOURS' This creamy-white, highly fragrant double variety has large domed blooms that glow the softest shade of yellow when fully open. This is my all-time favorite white peony.

'RASPBERRY SUNDAE' The name is perfectly fitting for this novelty variety that sports massive, ultraruffled pink flower heads that sit atop a lovely cup of wide-flaring creamy petals. To me, it looks like a big scoop of vanilla ice cream dripping with raspberry jam. It is a wonderful cut flower with a sweet, mild fragrance.

VASE LIFE TRICKS

Peonies make wonderful, long-lasting cut flowers that generally persist for over a week. You can pick them as open as you like, but for the best vase life, harvest them while in bud. I aim for harvesting at the "soft marshmallow" stage—in the mornings I go through the plants and gently squeeze each flower bud, feeling for sponginess. If buds are still hard, then I leave them to ripen longer, but if they feel soft—similar to a marshmallow—I pick them. When harvesting, be sure to leave at least 2 sets of leaves on the stem so that the plant can continue to grow and store food over the summer.

'CORAL CHARM'

'BOWL OF BEAUTY'

'RASPBERRY SUNDAE'

Cut stems can also be stored for later use; they will last for 2 to 3 weeks in the refrigerator. When storing, remove almost all of the leaves; bunch the stems together, and slip them into a plastic bag with a few paper towels inside to absorb any excess moisture. Lay flat on the shelf in the produce area of the fridge and then check them every few days for signs of mold. Discard any that begin to rot. Upon removal, the flowers often look limp, but don't worry. Recut the stems and place them immediately in warm water with flower preservative. The buds will open within 24 hours, and the blooms will last a good week in the vase.

RANUNCULUSES

If I had to choose only one flower to grow in our hoop houses each spring, hands down, it would be ranunculuses. With so many wonderful qualities—tall stems, double ruffled blooms, a light citrusy rose fragrance, high productivity, and one of the widest color ranges imaginable—it is impossible not to fall head over heels for these beauties.

HOW TO GROW

Unlike many of the other flowers profiled in this book, ranunculuses are actually quite tender. In areas with low temps of 10° to 20°F (-12.3° to -6.6°C) or higher, they can be successfully planted outdoors in autumn with minimal protection.

If you live in a very cold area, where temps dip well below freezing for extended periods of time, start ranunculuses in a hoop house or low tunnel at the very beginning of spring. Plant outside once you're sure the ground won't freeze—this is often about a month before your last spring frost. They won't be quite as prolific as autumn-started plants, but you'll still get a nice harvest.

Order corms in late summer for the best selection and for fall delivery. Always get the largest size available, 2 to 3 inches (5 to 7 cm); they will produce more abundantly and the flowers will be larger. Bigger corms will give 10 to 12 stems in a growing season, whereas smaller ones, 1 to 1½ inches (3 to 4 cm), will produce only 5 to 7 stems.

When it's planting time, soak the corms for 3 to 4 hours in room-temperature water. As the corms soak, they will plump up. After soaking, you can plant the corms directly into the ground or presprout them. Presprouting before planting in the ground will get the plants blooming 3 to 4 weeks earlier than non-presprouted ones, but you can skip this and still get adequate results.

To presprout, fill a flat-bottom seed tray half full with moist potting soil. Scatter the soaked corms over the soil and cover them with more soil so that they are completely covered. Leave this tray in a cool place— 50° to 55°F (10° to 12.7°C)—for 10 to 14 days. It is important to check them every week; make sure the soil is moist but not soggy, and remove any corms that show signs of rot or mold. During this time, the corms will swell to twice their original size and develop little white hairlike rootlets. Once these roots are ½ inch (1 cm) long (pull them up to check), plant them in the ground 1 inch (2.5 cm) deep, 8 inches (20 cm) apart, down the row.

Ranunculuses normally start to flower about 90 days after planting. Our late autumn–planted corms bloom in early spring and continue steadily for 6 to 7 weeks. When grown for cutting, they're best planted as an annual crop from new corms each year.

FAVORITE VARIETIES

I have had the best success with the La Belle Series, of which my top favorites are Salmon, Champagne, Orange, Pink Picotee, and the Pastel Mix.

VASE LIFE TRICKS

Ranunculuses have an outstanding vase life, often exceeding 10 days. Cut when buds are colored and squishy like a marshmallow, but not yet fully open, for a vase life of 10 to 12 days. If the blooms are open when cut, they'll still last a week but will be more fragile to transport.

SWEET PEAS

When I was a little girl, I spent summers in the country and spent a lot of time visiting my great-grandparents. One of my jobs was to keep fresh flowers by my Grammy's bedside table. She had a number of beautiful bloomers growing in her garden, but the ones that I remember most are the tangle of rainbow-colored sweet peas climbing up her carport posts. When my husband and I bought our first house, the very first thing I planted was a huge tunnel of sweet peas right in the center of the garden. That spring, as the first flowers opened, their scent transported me back in time to the summers of my youth and the happy memories of picking flowers in Grammy's garden. I've been growing sweet peas for over 10 years now, and each spring as they climb their trellises, it's like seeing my dear old friends once again.

HOW TO GROW

There are three main types of sweet peas, grouped by their bloom time. Depending on your climate and desired harvest window, you can choose from the following:

- Winter flowering: These include the Winter Elegance and Winter Sunshine Series, which flower earliest of all. The key is that you need around 10 hours of daylight, and protection from frost. If you plant in the autumn, they will flower by midwinter in warmer, southern parts of the United States like Texas and California or in other toasty parts of the world like South Africa, Australia, and mild areas of Japan. For those in regions with less winter sunlight and/or colder temperatures, grow these varieties in a hoop house where they can thrive inside and flower in the earliest months of spring.

- Spring flowering: These include the midseason grandiflora varieties like Mammoth and the Spring Sunshine Series, which will begin to flower with around 11 hours of daylight and roughly 2 weeks after the winter types.

- Summer flowering: This group includes the Spencer varieties, which start to flower with around 12 hours of daylight. They are by far the most popular worldwide. The Spencers are heat tolerant, produce abundant long stems, come in a dizzying rainbow of colors, and are generally the easiest of all the groups to grow—especially perfect for beginners.

In warmer regions where winter weather is mild, sow sweet peas in autumn. Everywhere else, sow in later winter/early spring. Soak your seeds for 24 hours before sowing. This softens the seed coat and speeds the sprouting process by a few days. While the seeds are soaking, fill your planting pots with soil. Sweet peas produce a ton of roots even in the beginning, so the more room you can give them during the early stages of life, the better they will grow in the long run. I always choose the deepest pots I can scrounge up, which are usually 4 inches (10 cm) wide and deep, and plant 2 seeds per pot.

While waiting for the seeds to sprout, prepare their growing beds. Sweet peas require a little extra pampering to produce abundantly. In addition to the standard soil preparation detailed in "Digging In" (page 27), I also run a 1-foot (30-cm) deep trench down the center of the bed and fill it with compost or well-rotted manure so that, once the sweet peas send their roots down deep, there is a feast awaiting them below. Then I put in a row of trellis supports (either wood or metal posts)

'VALERIE HARROD'

'RESTORMEL'

'MOLLIE RILSTONE'

'JILLY'

'CHARLIE'S ANGEL'

'NIMBUS'

roughly 8 feet apart down the row and attach 6-foot (1.8-m) tall metal fencing (such as chicken wire) for the flowers to climb up. Finally, I lay down soaker hoses to run alongside the seedlings, because sweet peas love water; without the hoses, keeping their thirst quenched during warm weather can become a full-time chore.

I set out seedlings around the time of the last spring frost in 2 rows, one on either side of the trellis, roughly 8 inches (20 cm) apart down the row, and for the first 6 weeks I give them a weekly dose of fish emulsion and kelp. Once the vines explode into lush growth, I stop. Keeping them tied to the trellis is important for straight stems, so every week I go through the patch and secure the plants to the metal fencing with twine. Once the vines get going, you can expect over 1 foot (30 cm) of growth a week, so be sure to stay on top of tying.

FAVORITE VARIETIES

Over the years, I have conducted numerous sweet pea trials, growing and testing close to a hundred different varieties, including both heirloom and hybrid types. While all have been beautiful, this handful contains the ones I just can't live without. All are Spencer types and bloom from late spring through midsummer in my garden.

'CHARLIE'S ANGEL' The massive, light icy-blue blossoms of this variety have made it one of the most popular on the show benches in England.

'JILLY' Winner of numerous awards, this variety's blooms are the loveliest shade of cream, and it's one of the finest garden varieties available.

'MOLLIE RILSTONE' This variety is the best of its color, with creamy, blush-tinted blooms that have a strong fruity scent, atop long, tall stems.

'NIMBUS' This is probably the most unique variety I've ever grown. The inky gray, eggplant-streaked blooms are a real conversation starter with everyone who visits our garden.

'RESTORMEL' The brilliant scarlet-cerise petals of this large-flowered variety will stop you in your tracks. It is excellent for cutting and highly fragrant.

'VALERIE HARROD' The petals of this variety are a brilliant glowing orange-pink, resembling unripe watermelon. It is vigorous and fragrant.

VASE LIFE TRICKS

Once the vines begin producing flowers, keeping up with the harvest can be tricky. I comb the rows every other morning so that I catch flowers at their prime. For the longest vase life, pick stems that have at least 2 unopened flowers at the tip. While they can be picked when more open, their vase life won't be quite as long. Sweet peas are a short-lived cut flower, lasting at best 4 to 5 days in a vase. Adding sugar or flower preservative to the water makes a big difference and will add a few extra days.

TULIPS

Our farm is located in the Skagit Valley, Washington, one of the largest tulip bulb–producing regions in the United States. Each spring, as the surrounding fields burst into a riot of colors, over a million visitors flock to our area for the Skagit Valley Tulip Festival. During a recent visit to one of the big display gardens at a local tulip farm, I was struck by just how many different choices there are in this one single family of plants. Blooms are available in every color, including black. They are borne on short stocky stems and tall thin ones. Some have fringed petals, others have pointed ones, and some are so ruffled and full that they are commonly mistaken for peonies. Some varieties carry a soft, subtle scent.

With so many wonderful qualities, it's no wonder that tulips are one of the most popular cut flowers. During the mid-17th century, Dutch citizens went crazy for them, and for a brief window of time, single bulbs reportedly sold for more than ten times an average person's salary. While that craze was short lived, tulips have remained extremely popular ever since.

HOW TO GROW

One of the easiest spring bulbs you can grow, tulips are a mainstay in the spring cutting garden. They require at least 6 weeks of cold weather to flower properly, so if you live where winters don't get down to freezing temperatures, opt for prechilled bulbs. Tulips do well in most soil types, as long as it's freely draining—standing water in heavy soils will cause bulbs to rot. Plant in fall in a spot that will get full sun, and place bulbs three times as deep as they are tall. Because we grow intensively, I place our bulbs very close together in the trench, similar to how eggs look in a carton. I recommend this approach because it encourages the stems to stretch and also allows many flowers to grow in a small amount of space.

FAVORITE VARIETIES

I've grown nearly a hundred different tulip varieties over the years, and while all have been beautiful, I find myself coming back to this little handful of treasures that not only perform well in the garden but also put on an amazing display in the vase.

'BRIGHT RED PARROT' One of the most notable parrot types I've seen ("parrot" describes a group of tulips with flamboyantly colored petals that are feathered, curled, twisted, or waved), this tomato soup–red variety has thick stems loaded with multiple blooms, which open to the size of a dessert plate when fully mature.

'CHARMING BEAUTY' My all-time favorite tulip, this egg yolk–yellow beauty opens to a ruffled double bloom that resembles a garden rose or peony.

'PROFESSOR RONTGEN' The largest parrot type I've ever grown, this variety has thick, tall stems topped with show-stopping, palm-sized orange blooms. The green-streaked, tangerine petals surround a cheerful yellow throat, making a bold, unforgettable statement.

'ROCOCO' The petals of this award-winning variety are a most unusual combination of cardinal red with deep purple and apple-green feathering.

'YELLOW POMPONETTE' This ultraruffled, school bus–yellow variety has unique coloring, including a striking black-flecked throat that offsets the petals perfectly.

'CHARMING BEAUTY'

'ROCOCO'

'YELLOW POMPONETTE'

'PROFESSOR RONTGEN'

'BRIGHT RED PARROT'

VASE LIFE TRICKS

Tulips are naturally a very long-lasting cut flower. Store-bought stems generally persist for 4 to 5 days, but homegrown varieties can easily hold for a week and a half in the vase. For the longest display inside, harvest when the flowers are still in bud with just a hint of color showing on the outer petals. Because tulips have a tendency to bend and curve right after harvest, wrap the top two-thirds of the flowers in a funnel of paper and stand them upright in water for a few hours. Once fully hydrated, they will stand much straighter in the vase. Keep in mind that once placed in water, fresh-picked stems will elongate during the first few days, so if you're adding them to an arrangement, nestle the flowers down deeper than you ultimately want them to be. Flower preservative will prolong the vase life of tulips and keep the petals vibrant and richly colored.

Spring
Projects

LILAC INFUSION

There's no better way to celebrate spring's abundance than by creating an overflowing arrangement filled with flowering branches and brilliant greens. During the short window that lilacs are in season, one must seize any opportunity to incorporate their heady blooms into daily life. From a few small stems on the bedside table to a massive statement piece that will fill a space with fragrance for days, the only rule is to bring as many indoors as possible.

Because lilacs are such a showstopping flower, I love making arrangements that highlight their beauty and stature, and also accentuate their vivid coloring. For this bouquet, I combine chartreuse snowball viburnum foliage with a mix of deep purple and black tulips, plus dusky purple hellebore seed heads and black fritillaria for a truly striking display.

YOU WILL NEED

A medium-sized French flower bucket

Pruners to use as needed while arranging

8 to 10 stems of snowball viburnum

6 stems of dark purple lilacs

8 stems of light purple or blue lilacs

12 to 15 stems of black and deep purple parrot and double tulips

10 stems of dusky purple hellebores

3 stems of *Fritillaria persica*

1 Fill the bucket with cool water and floral preservative before starting. Place the viburnum stems in the flower bucket, working to space them as evenly as possible. These will establish the overall shape of your arrangement.

2 Once the base structure of greens is in place, add the lilacs. Beginning with the darker colored blooms, fill in all of the large open spots throughout the arrangement.

3 Next, add the light purple or blue varieties, snuggling them in next to the dark ones.

4 To add more depth to the mix of purples in the arrangement, incorporate the striking black and purple tulips. To keep these smaller flowers from getting lost in the massive sea of bloom, cluster them in groups of 3, and place them evenly throughout the arrangement.

5 Thread the dusky purple hellebores among the other foliage and flowers, especially toward the front of the bouquet. Finish off the arrangement by tucking in the black fritillaria. These unique flowers will make the entire arrangement pop.

SPRING FLOWER CROWN

There's nothing quite like a crown of fresh blooms to put you in a celebratory mood. These floral accessories are no longer seen only at weddings—a flower crown can be worn to just about any special occasion.

All you need to create one of these pretty halos is a few handfuls of flowers and greens and some basic floral supplies. Once you learn how easy they are to make, you'll likely be making crowns for you and all your friends.

YOU WILL NEED

2 feet (60 cm) of paper-covered wire

Ten 6-inch (15-cm) pieces of floral or paddle wire

A roll of floral tape

6 to 8 feet (1.8 to 2.4 m) of decorative ribbon

2 stems of viburnum, with 8 to 10 blossoms removed

12 stems of muscari

9 or 10 stems of ranunculus

1 stem of Canterbury bells (*Campanula medium*), 8 blossoms removed

8 to 10 small stems of larkspur

1 Determine the crown's diameter by wrapping the paper-covered wire around your head where you want it to sit. Leave a few extra inches/centimeters on either end for fastening together later. Make a loop on one end and leave the other straight. (After fitting the crown to your head, straighten it out before adding materials.)

2 For large, heavy blooms like ranunculus that need extra support, wire the stems individually for added stability before securing them to the bundles. Make a hairpin with floral wire and slip it gently down through the center of the flower head. Then tape the wire and stem together.

3 Put together mini bouquets of roughly 4 to 6 stems each, using a mixture of the listed greens and blooms. I generally use 8 to 10 mini bouquets for an average-sized crown. For a delicate crown, make the bundles petite; for a fuller finished piece, make the bundles bigger. Cut the stem ends so that 2 to 3 inches (5 to 8 cm) of stem are remaining.

4 Wrap each mini bouquet's stems together with floral tape, starting at the base and going around each mini bouquet until the stems are fully covered. Floral tape gets sticky when gently stretched, so be sure to pull on it slightly as you work, and it will adhere to itself.

5 To build the crown, take one of the mini bouquets and lay it along the paper-covered wire. Wrap floral tape around the mini bouquet and the wire a few times until it's thoroughly attached.

6 Add the remaining mini bouquets, facing them in the same direction as the first and placing them so that each hides the previous mini bouquet's stem ends, until the paper-covered wire base is covered.

8 Place the crown on your head and secure the two ends together by looping the straight end of the wire through the loop on the other side and twisting to secure it.

9 If you won't be wearing the crown right away, store it in the produce area of your refrigerator for up to 2 days to keep it fresh.

7 After all of the flowers are attached, tie a few pieces of ribbon on either side of the clasp in the back.

SHERBET BUTTERFLY BOUQUET FOR MOM

One of my favorite color palettes to work with is a mix of warm sherbet tones of peach, coral, apricot, tangerine, and salmon. Each spring, as the papery Iceland poppies start to unfurl from their fuzzy buds and the citrus-scented ranunculus make their debut, it's impossible not to heap them all together into one giant, ruffled, ultraromantic bouquet.

To offset the warm tones, and to keep the bouquet from becoming overly sweet, mix in some rich, dark foliage along with a few hits of bright acid green. The deep copper hues of the ornamental plum leaves paired with the bright chartreuse seedpods of the mature hellebores work beautifully together and balance the entire arrangement.

YOU WILL NEED

1 medium terra-cotta vase

Pruners to use as needed while arranging

6 long arching stems of dark plum foliage

6 long arching hawthorn branches in bud

6 stems of lacy viburnum in flower, leaves removed

8 stems of chartreuse hellebores

20 large peach and coral Iceland poppies

15 peach and pale yellow ranunculus

1 Fill the vase with water and floral preservative before starting. Establish a strong framework for the bouquet by placing 2 arching stems of plum foliage so that they hang out over the right side of the vase. Then place 2 more so that they lean out over the left side of the vase, to provide balance. Then add 2 tall, towering stems to the back left corner of the vase. The goal here is to create an off-center, upside-down tripod shape that will give the completed arrangement a beautiful cascading, slightly asymmetrical look.

2 Following the same overall shape established by the plum stems, weave in the hawthorn and then the viburnum, making the branches arch and cascade as much as possible.

3 Fill in any empty holes with the hellebores. Use the most arching stems around the lip of the vase, to accentuate the overall loose shape.

4 Thread in the Iceland poppies among the other stems. Pay close attention to their natural stem shapes and place the curviest stems on the outside edges, again echoing the foliage framework. Turn some of the flower faces upward and some facing out to the sides, so that you can see the unique, crinkled qualities of the petals and the centers of these amazing blooms.

5 Place the ranunculus in among the poppies to tie it all together. The final arrangement will resemble a vase full of colorful butterflies resting on the leaves of a tree.

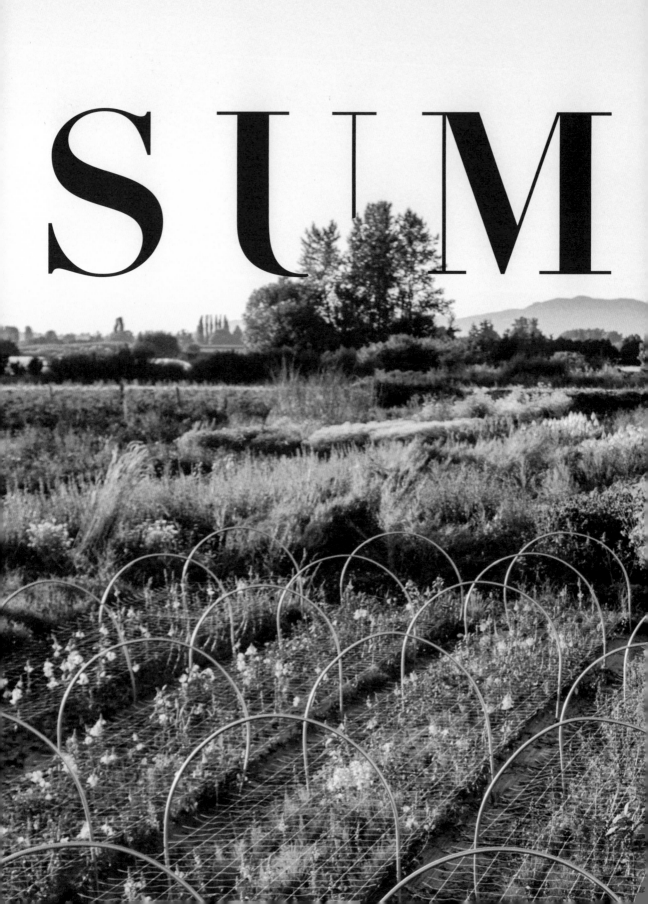

MER

WELCOMING THE
ABUNDANCE

Summer on the farm is always such a busy time. I rise when the rooster crows, long before dawn, and spend nearly every daylight hour working in the garden. The warm temperatures and long days quickly transform the once-manageable flower patch into a jungle of waist-high weeds, foliage, and blooms. Each week it feels like I'm stepping into a new garden because everything is growing so rapidly. Sunflowers grow more than a foot a week, vines scramble up and over their trellises, and dahlias transform from little brown tubers into big, beefy plants in just a couple of months.

As the season progresses, my focus shifts away from sowing seeds and planting to weeding, staking, monitoring for bugs and disease, and harvesting wave after wave of flowers. All of my winter planning and spring preparation come to life, and there's no more beautiful or abundant time of year.

It takes a serious amount of focus and effort to keep on top of everything. You won't find me complaining, though, because to me there is nothing more stunning or rewarding than wading through a field of flowers in full, rolling bloom.

Summer
Tasks

PLANT SUMMER FLOWERS

During the first part of the season, planting tender young seedlings of summer flowers, bulbs, and tubers is an ongoing weekly task. I plant successions of all of the warm weather lovers, including basil, celosia, gomphrena, and zinnias, and others from seed through the first month of summer, and I start super-fast-growing crops—like single stem sunflowers, which will bloom just 60 days after seeding—through midsummer, since they will mature before the cold fall weather arrives.

SOW BIENNIALS

These prolific spring bloomers (see "Biennials" on page 59) require a full year to mature and flower. Sow seeds (using seed trays) in early summer and get plants into the ground during mid- to late summer, a good 6 to 8 weeks before the first fall frost, so that they have time to establish fully before cold weather sets in.

WATER

Plants need three things to thrive: sunlight, fertile soil, and adequate water. During the summer months, as temperatures rise, keeping the garden hydrated with watering by hand can become a full-time task. Even if you are tending a tiny plot, setting up some type of watering system such as drip irrigation or soaker hoses will save you many hours and dollars (and anxiety) over the course of a year. Compared to overhead sprinklers, drip irrigation uses 25 percent less water, concentrating the moisture at the root zone rather than on the leaves, where it can easily evaporate on a warm day and also encourage foliar diseases. Flowering plants require regular watering of at least 1 inch (2.5 cm) of water per week to maintain good health and steady growth.

STAKE, TRELLIS, AND TIE UP

Plants remind me of young children, because they can shoot up a couple of inches almost overnight. Keeping this vigorous growth corralled is extremely important. A heavy rain or a gusty day can turn a lush patch of flowers into a soggy, toppled-over mess in a matter of hours. In my garden, I use a good deal of flower netting, along with sturdy metal stakes and lots of baling twine, to keep plants upright. For a detailed overview of my favorite plant staking techniques, see "Supporting Your Flowers" on page 36.

PINCH

It can be hard for new flower growers to embrace this technique, which involves cutting back the growth of a young plant and delaying its flowering for a few weeks, because it seems counterintuitive. But in my experience, pinching back greatly increases yields and extends the harvest window of plants that produce several rounds of bloom. When plants are young, generally with just 3 to 5 sets of true leaves, use sharp pruners to snip off the top of the plant before it has a chance to set a flower bud. This stimulates the plant to branch, which means sending up many more stems from the base. Not all varieties benefit from this practice, but those that naturally branch—like amaranth, celosia, cosmos, dahlias, snapdragons, and zinnias—all do. I've done comparisons with both dahlias and zinnias, pinching some plants and not others. The pinched plants produced much longer stems, over a much greater span of time, often producing double the yield of an unpinched plant.

KEEP WEEDING

One of my least favorite tasks but also one of the most important, weeding needs to be done regularly in summer; otherwise, the garden will turn into a jungle-like mess overnight. Try to catch weeds while they are young and easy to remove, or you will be stuck with hours of backbreaking work that would have taken just minutes a few weeks before. During the summer months, I spend an hour each evening with a collinear hoe, lightly cultivating the soil around young plants so that the weeds stay in check.

HARVEST AND DEADHEAD

Keeping on top of the summer crop is a big job. I comb through the garden at least three times a week, grabbing flowers at their peak, because this will ensure the longest vase life and also keep the garden producing abundantly. Once flowers set seed, they will slow down and eventually stop blooming. To extend your harvest, prune off spent flowers, anything that's damaged, or those you missed when harvesting, often—this will encourage plants to send up new growth and flower stalks over a longer period of time.

126

ORDER BULBS

It always feels very odd to be ordering winter- and spring-blooming bulbs during the height of summer, but I've learned the hard way that it pays to order as early as possible to get the best selection. If you dillydally, you will miss out on your favorite varieties. Order spring-blooming bulbs before midsummer, and preorder paperwhites and amaryllises anytime in summer, for fall delivery.

ORDER HARDY ANNUAL SEED

Be sure to order fresh seed for plants like larkspur, love-in-a-mist, and false Queen Anne's lace for planting in fall.

MANAGE PESTS AND DISEASE

It's supremely discouraging to walk out into the garden to find your precious flowers being nibbled on by some mysterious bug, or even worse, their tender leaves covered in spots or a powdery film. Every region deals with a different set of insects and diseases, so I encourage you to find resources in your area—such as nurseries, garden clubs, or Master Gardener groups—that can help you identify and treat problems that are common to where you live.

No matter where you garden, a few key practices can help prevent problems. Plants, like people, get sick when they are under stress, and I've found that if any part of my garden suffers from prolonged stress, insects and disease move in shortly thereafter. So be sure to water, weed, and check for bugs and diseases regularly. Remove sickly plants at once and dispose of them in the burn pile or trash, since disease spores don't always die in the compost pile. By spotting insects early, you can take swift measures before the problem gets out of hand.

Summer Blooms, Edibles & Foliage

COSMOS

Of all the annual plants you can grow in your cutting garden, none is more productive than cosmos. They truly are a cut-and-come-again flower: the more you harvest them, the more they bloom. A single planting will produce buckets and buckets of airy, delicate, daisylike blossoms for many months. You can arrange them on their own or weave them into mixed bouquets. The possibilities are endless.

HOW TO GROW

There really is no easier plant to start and grow than cosmos. Sow seeds about 4 weeks before the last spring frost, then plant seedlings into the garden once all danger of frost has passed. Be careful not to sow seed too early, because seedlings will quickly outgrow their pots before the weather has warmed enough to put them out into the garden.

These plants get very bushy and prefer a little extra room to spread out, so space plants 12 to 18 inches (30 to 46 cm) apart. Once in the ground, cosmos will grow rapidly, so be sure to stake or net them early, while they are still young. Cosmos also benefit from pinching, as this will encourage the already highly productive plants to branch even more vigorously. I do this when plants are 12 inches (30 cm) tall, taking out the top few sets of leaves. To prolong their flowering time, keep cosmos harvested and deadheaded regularly, before they set seed.

FAVORITE VARIETIES

I typically do two sowings, a month apart, and list some of my favorites here. This gives me a wide range of flower types and loads of blooms for cutting from summer into fall.

DOUBLE CLICK MIX This unique double-flowered cosmos has fluffy blooms that look smashing in bouquets. As well as being available in a mix, it also comes in single colors, including clean white Snow Puff, vibrant maroon Cranberries, rosy mauve Rose Bonbon, and lovely soft blush Bicolor Pink.

PIED PIPER SERIES A seashell-type bloomer with fluted petals, this series comes in individual colors. Red is a beautiful deep maroon and Blush White is a soft, creamy blush pink.

'PURITY' This cheerful daisylike bloomer has perfect, pure white single flowers.

'RUBENZA' The darkest colored cosmos on the market, this bold choice has flowers that change from bright ruby red to dark rose as they mature.

SEASHELLS MIX These uniquely shaped flowers with tubular petals create a stunning three-dimensional display. The mix includes various shades of pink, blush, and white.

VERSAILLES MIX This early blooming, vigorous mix includes the loveliest blend of daisylike flowers in white, mauve, pink, and burgundy. It's one of the fastest to bloom from seed—flowering in about 2 months after planting—and one of the most prolific mixes on the market.

VASE LIFE TRICKS

The individual blooms of cosmos don't last a particularly long time in the vase, about 4 to 6 days, but each stem is loaded with multiple blossoms that open individually over a period of a week. Harvest when the buds are colored but haven't opened up yet; this will keep insects from pollinating them and help stretch the vase life by a few additional days. Use floral preservative in the vase water.

VERSAILLES MIX

DOUBLE CLICK MIX

PIED PIPER SERIES

'PURITY'

SEASHELLS MIX

'RUBENZA'

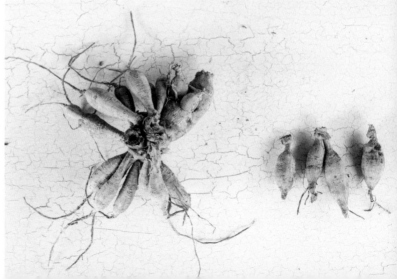

DAHLIAS

———

I get asked all the time what my favorite flower is, and answering always feels a little like singling out a favorite child. In truth, I could never really choose a favorite; however, during the late months of summer I almost always say dahlias. Over the years, I have trialed and tested over 450 varieties and now grow between 3,000 and 4,000 dahlia plants for cut flower production each summer.

Because dahlias are easy to grow, come in a rainbow of colors, are nearly unmatched in terms of production, and have flowers in a range of shapes that resemble daisies, peonies, and even water lilies, I love this plant family more every year. Whether you have a small cutting garden or a large flower farm, you'll definitely want to include a few of these beautiful, versatile, and productive plants in the mix.

HOW TO GROW

Grow dahlias in full sun. Because they're extremely cold sensitive, it is important to wait to plant them until the ground has warmed to 60°F (15.5°C), normally about 2 weeks after your last spring frost. Lay tubers in planting holes horizontally, 4 to 6 inches (10 to 15 cm) deep, and do not water until they sprout up through the soil. I grow them in double rows in beds that are 3 feet (1 m) wide, spacing plants 18 inches (46 cm) apart.

Once any foliage emerges from the ground, water deeply 2 or 3 times a week for at least 30 minutes. After plants reach 1 foot (30 cm) tall, give them a hard pinch by snipping out 3 to 4 (7.5 to 10 cm) inches of the growing center to encourage low basal branching and increased stem count, and longer overall stem length.

Slugs and snails are dahlias' number one enemy. Put down bait about 2 weeks after planting, or as soon as you see foliage emerging from the ground, and then periodically through the season. I use Sluggo, an organic option that's safe for both children and pets.

By midsummer, plants will get tall and require staking to keep them from falling over. I recommend the corral method, which involves placing a metal T-post every 10 feet (3 m) along the outside of the beds and then stringing a double layer of baling twine from post to post to corral the plants in. For home gardeners with just a few plants, place tall, sturdy posts next to tubers at planting time so you can tie stems to them as they grow.

In most areas, winters are too cold to leave tubers in the ground to perennialize, so after blooming, you need to dig them up and store them. After a few frosts in the fall, lift the tuber clumps out of the ground with a pitchfork, being careful not to slice through the clumps as you go. Wash the clumps to remove all of the excess soil. (I use a strong hose to do this.) Then dip the clumps into a 5-percent bleach-water solution and lay them out to dry in a cool garage or basement for a day or two.

I advise dividing dahlias every year, because their tubers grow quickly, and when they get too large they can rot or become too heavy to lift and store. Once the clumps have dried after washing, split them in half with sharp pruners so you're left with two smaller, more workable pieces. Then divide the halved clumps into individual tubers. For a viable tuber, it is essential that the eye or eyes (swollen growing nodes) are connected to a complete, unbroken tuber. If you accidentally break one, just toss it.

135

'PUNKIN SPICE'

'AMBER QUEEN'

'CRICHTON HONEY'

'SNOHO DORIS'

'APPLEBLOSSOM'

'CAFÉ AU LAIT'

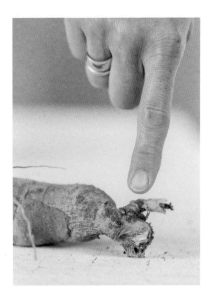

In my early growing days I tried to save many of these, but they always ended up rotting; it's better to be ruthless on the front end. With a little practice it gets pretty easy to spot eyes and separate tubers with accuracy and speed. After dividing, store the tubers in a medium such as slightly dampened peat moss or sawdust in a newspaper-lined box, or wrap them individually in pieces of plastic cling wrap. Keep them in a cool, dry area with a temperature of 40° to 50°F (4° to 10°C), such as a basement or garage for the winter. Check monthly throughout the winter, and toss any that show signs of rot.

FAVORITE VARIETIES

'AMBER QUEEN' This adorable little warm orange, button-flowered novelty is a welcome addition to any bouquet. Its compact plant stature, miniature flower heads, and good garden performance make it a longtime favorite.

'APPLEBLOSSOM' The delicate, saucer-sized blooms on this buttercream-blush beauty make it a must-grow for any flower arranger. In addition to holding very well in the vase, it performs excellently in the garden.

'CAFÉ AU LAIT' Few flowers can compare to the sheer beauty of this massive, creamy beige–blush pink dinner plate dahlia. One of the most popular summer wedding bouquet requests, this variety is a must-grow.

'CRICHTON HONEY' The large glowing apricot-peach, ball-shaped flowers on this highly productive plant are some of the most well loved in my garden.

'PUNKIN SPICE' The fluffy, warm orange-gold-raspberry petals of this winning variety make it an unforgettable addition to any bouquet. Many of the blooms look almost like they were tie-dyed, with no two the same. The stems are thin, so be sure to give them a little extra support in the garden; otherwise, they can get damaged in heavy rains.

'SNOHO DORIS' A warm blend of peachy pink and soft orange, this brilliant ball-shaped variety has strong stems that are perfect for cutting and last in the vase.

VASE LIFE TRICKS

While dahlias are not a terribly long-lasting cut flower, you can get 5 to 7 days from stems picked at the proper stage. Since dahlias don't unfurl much after they've been harvested, it's important to pick them almost fully open but at the same time not overly ripe. Check the back of each flower head, looking for firm and lush petals; papery or slightly dehydrated ones signal old age. Use floral preservative in the water.

138

FRAGRANT LEAVES

Having a steady supply of foliage is key to successfully making bouquets during the long months of summer, and a few stems of any of these fragrant-leaved varieties will add perfume to your arrangements and bouquets. I cut these mainly for foliage, and I harvest so often that they don't get a chance to flower. You can also use them in bloom, though the flowers aren't particularly impressive.

FAVORITE VARIETIES

BASIL With a spicy, licorice-like scent, basil is one of the most fragrant, easy to grow, and abundant summer foliage plants. 'Oriental Breeze' is the most handsome variety of all, sporting deep purple flowers, glossy foliage, and a fantastic scent. 'Cinnamon', 'Lemon', and purple-leaved types like 'Aromato' are wonderful workhorses, too. **How to grow:** Plants are easy to start from seed; they should be protected from cool weather in the spring, so don't set them outside until all danger of frost has passed. (In our cool climate, basil must be grown in low tunnels to lessen disease pressure and extend the stem length.) Space plants 1 foot (30 cm) apart in a spot that gets all-day sun. To produce stems that are great in bouquets, pinch (see page 126) early, when plants are 8 to 12 inches (20 to 30 cm) tall. **Vase life tricks:** Once cut, basil foliage is prone to wilting in the heat, so harvest in the cool of the morning or evening and place in water to rest for a few hours before arranging. Stems will last for 7 to 10 days, often rooting in the vase. No floral preservative is needed.

BEE BALM (*Monarda* hybrid 'Lambada') While all kinds of *Monarda* are very productive, this annual variety is even more notable than the perennials. The plant is easy to grow from seed in spring, has wonderfully scented foliage that smells like Earl Grey tea, and holds well in arrangements; it can be succession planted throughout the summer, and it churns out an enormous amount of volume from even the smallest planting. Its unusual overall coloring—a mix of green, gray, and soft purple—and the whorl-shaped blooms make it more useful as a filler plant like bells of Ireland than as an actual flower. **How to grow:** Plants are easy to start from seed; they should be protected from cool weather in the spring, so don't set them outside until all danger of frost has passed. Bee balm gets quite large, so set plants 18 inches (46 cm) apart, with 2 to 3 rows per bed. **Vase life tricks:** Pick when the flower whorls begin to turn from all green to purple. These flowers are prone to wilting in the heat, so harvest in the cool of the morning or evening and place in water to rest for a few hours before arranging. Stems will persist for 7 to 10 days if you use floral preservative.

140

MINT I was advised to never plant this vigorous spreader but am so glad I didn't listen. Mint is one of the first foliage plants available to harvest in the spring and makes early spring bouquets possible. My favorite kinds are apple mint, peppermint, white variegated pineapple mint, and spearmint. **How to grow:** Grow in full sun to part shade, starting plants in either spring (in cold climates) or autumn when varieties are available in nurseries, in a place where they can wander without causing any trouble. If you don't want it to spread, tuck plants into large pots or a whiskey barrel planter. **Vase life tricks:** Pick stems when they're mature and have become firm, and they'll last for well over a week, sometimes even rooting in the vase. No floral preservative is needed.

SCENTED GERANIUM (*Pelargonium*) These make an amazing foliage base for arrangements from midsummer to late autumn. I adore 'Attar of Roses', 'Chocolate Mint', 'Ginger', and 'Lemon Fizz'—they smell just as their names indicate. **How to grow:** Start from plants in spring, after any danger of frost has passed. 'Chocolate Mint' is worthy of special mention: with large leaves splashed with burgundy veins, it is hands down my favorite geranium variety. If left to grow, its stems can easily reach 3 feet (1 m), making them perfect for large bouquets. Space all scented geranium plants 1 foot (30 cm) apart in full sun. I grow mine under a low tunnel—the added heat encourages lush, vigorous growth and allows me to plant them earlier in the season and keep harvesting up until the first hard frost in autumn. **Vase life tricks:** For best results, it's essential to delay harvest until the plants have matured enough for the stems to harden up a bit. Otherwise, they'll wilt and won't recover after harvest. Pick in the early morning or in the cool of the evening, then place them right in water and let them rest in a cool spot for a few hours. These stems will often last more than a week in the vase if floral preservative is used.

BASIL

BEE BALM

MINT

SCENTED GERANIUM

FRUITS & FOLIAGE

Offering varied texture and beautiful coloring, cuttings from shrubs and trees strategically complement your focal flowers and help make any floral design shine. I stock the garden with a large supply of these hardworking backbone plants; the following list offers a bounty from late spring through early autumn.

HOW TO GROW

The following deciduous trees and shrubs are easy to grow and thrive in most climates. Choose a spot in full sun with well-draining soil, making sure to give plants plenty of room to stretch out as they grow. The best time to plant is during the fall, if you're planting in potted plants, and winter if you're planting bare-root shrubs.

FAVORITE VARIETIES

BEECH (*Fagus sylvatica*) In terms of harvesting foliage, beech is one of the most useful trees I've ever worked with. In the first part of summer they might appear too tender to use, but they're actually remarkably hardy and can be used out of water with great success for both delicate wirework like boutonnieres and larger installations such as garlands and arbors. The 'Tricolor' variety is particularly lovely, with magenta leaves streaked with deep burgundy. By midsummer and into the autumn, the leaves on the copper beech become leathery and change from eggplant to a gorgeous rusty brown. This variety in particular beautifully complements late season arrangements and wreaths. New growth will easily last a week in a vase, and the leathery leaves of late summer will last twice that.

CRABAPPLE (*Malus* 'Evereste') An essential ingredient when blooming in spring, crabapples also shine from midsummer through late autumn when the tree produces perfect clusters of cherry-sized fruit; those of 'Evereste' change in color from green to pale orange to cranberry streaked to red over the course of the season. Remove most of the leaves before adding to an arrangement so that the fruit can be easily seen. Stems will last at least a week in the vase.

EUROPEAN HORNBEAM (*Carpinus betulus*) The prominent veins on the leaves of this variety appear almost corrugated or crimped and are a great addition to large arrangements. Though the foliage looks delicate and fresh, it holds amazingly well out of water and is a key ingredient in summer garlands and as the structural base for large-scale arrangements. Single leaves are also nice backings for boutonnieres. Foliage will persist from 7 to 10 days in the vase.

NINEBARK This is one of the most productive and hardworking shrubs you can grow for cutting. Beginning in late spring, plants produce flower-loaded stems that are ideal in early spring arrangements. Once the flowers fade, they leave behind little clusters of gorgeous seed cases, which accent bouquets with texture. Throughout the rest of the season, this shrub just keeps pumping out the foliage-laden stems. What makes this group of plants so special is that they come in a number of unusual colors rarely found elsewhere in the plant world: 'Diabolo' has nearly black foliage, 'Coppertina' and 'Summer Wine' both bear brownish burgundy-orange leaves, and for a chartreuse pop, 'Nugget' and 'Dart's Gold' are the answer. Foliage has a 10- to 14-day vase life if cut when the leaves are fully mature.

RASPBERRY GREENS

RASPBERRY GREENS | started using raspberry foliage in bouquets years ago, and it's still on my favorites list. The plants are wildly productive, providing foliage all summer long. The everbearing varieties like 'Summit' and golden are best for an extended harvest of fruiting stems, can be cut to the ground in the winter for easy cleanup, spread rapidly for increased stock, grow in poorer soil than traditional summer fruiting types, and fruit in red and yellow. The summer fruiting types such as 'Tulameen' offer beautiful fruited branches for 3 to 4 weeks and abundant foliage from late spring through autumn. The greens last over 2 weeks in the vase.

VASE LIFE TRICKS

Harvest these stems when it's cool in the morning or evening, and immediately strip the bottom third of the stems of their foliage. Then, using clippers, split the woody stem ends vertically a few inches/cm and place them in a bucket of cool, fresh water. Let them rest for a few hours before arranging. Using flower preservative in the water will help prolong the life of cut stems, but all of the varieties listed here are very hardy and long lasting.

CRABAPPLE

EUROPEAN HORNBEAM

NINEBARK

BEECH

LILIES

With towering stems and waxy, trumpet-shaped flowers, lilies are the queens of the early summer garden. They come in a dazzling range of colors, including red, orange, yellow, pink, white, and even almost black. Some have stripes or freckles on their petals; others have such a powerful scent that just one stem will fill a room with a musky fragrance for days. Lilies are easy to grow, thrive in most areas, and will come back year after year. I have grown close to 50 different lily varieties.

HOW TO GROW

Order lily bulbs in summer and plant them immediately upon receipt from early to mid-autumn. Lilies like full sun and well-drained soil. To plant the bulbs, dig a trench 6 to 8 inches (15 to 20 cm) deep and set the bulbs in, root side down, twice the bulb's width from each other. Fill in the trench with soil and compost or well-rotted manure and top off with a few inches (5 to 10 cm) of mulch to suppress weeds and insulate the bulbs in winter. Once new growth emerges in the spring, water regularly and keep the area weeded.

FAVORITE VARIETIES

There are many different groups of lilies, categorized by different traits. The following are the most widely grown, and flower for a few weeks each. Asiatic and Oriental lilies start blooming in earliest summer; OT hybrids and trumpet lilies start blooming in midsummer.

Asiatic lilies are the first to bloom; they are the most commonly grown type of lily in the commercial cut flower trade. Their flowers face upward, making them great additions to hand-tied mixed bouquets. They come in a rainbow of bright colors; the stems can bear up to a dozen flowers each, and they grow well just about anywhere. Asiatics are unscented, so if fragrance is a concern, give these a try.

Oriental lilies are by far the most fragrant group—one stem can fill an entire room with a sweet, musky scent for days—and also come in some of the most luxurious, saturated, vivid colors with the grandest star-shaped flowers.

OT hybrids, a cross between Oriental and trumpet lilies, are some of my favorites to grow and arrange because they are sweetly scented and come in a range of unusual, muted colors that make them especially easy to blend in floral designs. These beauties carry the very best qualities of each, with the coloring of the trumpets and scent of the Oriental lilies.

Trumpet lilies are dramatic, with plum-colored buds that give way to blooms in softer shades than Oriental or Asiatic types. Each year the flower stems get taller and more blossom laden, so plant new bulbs every few years in order to have manageable cut flowers to harvest. The scent of trumpet lilies is rich and sweet and hangs in the air on warm days. Once established, these plants will need some staking to stand up straight under the weight of the flower heads.

'CONCA D'OR' Few blooms can contend with this OT showstopper; its buttercream petals look as if they are glowing from the inside out. The fragrance of this flower is warm, sweet, and unforgettable.

'MONTEGO BAY' Probably my favorite OT lily, this one has burnt orange-raspberry petals with buttery yellow edges—one of the most pleasing color combinations nature's ever put together—and a clean, fruity fragrance.

149

'CONCA D'OR'

'PLAYTIME' The name perfectly describes this cheerful Oriental lily variety. The clean white flowers have unique stripes of yellow and cranberry and are speckled with little dots of raspberry. The flowers are highly fragrant, and the blooms will light up a room.

'SALTARELLO' These deep pink buds give way to warm cantaloupe-colored blooms, stunning in bouquets and alone in the vase. This OT hybrid will always have a place in my garden.

'SORBONNE' While the flowers of this Oriental variety are a simple rose pink, it's the thin white band around the edges, and the sugarlike fragrance, that get me every time. People often swear that they smell cotton candy when I put these in a bouquet!

VASE LIFE TRICKS

Lilies are an extremely long-lasting cut flower; it's not uncommon for them to bloom for at least 10 days in the vase. Pick them when the buds are colored and the bottom flower is just beginning to open. Lily pollen is very messy and will stain, so as soon as the blooms open, take a piece of tissue and pull off the pollen anthers. Using floral preservative in the water will help the petals retain their deep coloring from bud to full bloom.

'MONTEGO BAY'

'PLAYTIME'

'SALTARELLO'

'SORBONNE'

PERENNIALS

Having a good stock of perennial plants in your cutting garden will make for effortless early summer bouquets. I have a big corner of my garden devoted to these hardworking beauties, and I cut heavily from them in early summer. They perfectly fill the gap between late spring bulbs and flowers and the earliest of the summer annuals.

HOW TO GROW

Perennials are hard to start from seed, so it's best to start them from nursery plants. They grow quickly, so skip the large pots and instead go with smaller versions to save money. It's best to plant in early autumn, at least 4 weeks before the first fall frost, to give the plants a chance to settle in before cold weather arrives. They can also be planted in spring, but they will be much less productive in the first year than if they'd been planted the previous autumn. All of the plants listed here get quite big, so space them 12 to 18 inches (30 to 46 cm) apart for the best productivity.

Perennials generally take 2 to 3 years to mature, so it's important to select a good site and keep weeds under control early on. After planting in autumn, I spread a thick layer of mulch over the beds to help keep weed seeds from germinating, then monitor them closely and stay on top of weeds in the spring.

FAVORITE VARIETIES

DELPHINIUM A big jug filled with mixed blue and purple delphiniums in the center of a room makes a regal statement. After a few years in the garden, these towering giants can get 5 to 6 feet tall (1.6 to 2 m). Since these plants grow quickly and are difficult to net or stake once they get growing, set up a solid support system for them early in the spring. I use a double layer of flower netting attached to metal posts to hold up large delphinium blooms. Of the dozens of cultivars available, I prefer the towering, double-flowered Pacific Giant Series; its blooms come in pale blue, cobalt, white, lavender, and mauve and have both black and white "bees" (the fluffy center in the throat of each flower). For gardeners who want shorter-stemmed blooms, the Magic Fountain Series is a great choice; it includes blooms in white, violet, and different shades of blue. **Vase life tricks:** Harvest when one-fourth to one-third of the flowers on a stem are open. If placed in water with floral preservative, delphiniums will last for 6 to 8 days in the vase.

PHLOX This cottage garden staple is nice and low maintenance. It comes in a wide range of colors, has large flower heads, and blooms prolifically for the first part of summer. Once the weather warms up, many get hit with powdery mildew, but I've never treated it, and the flowers have never seemed too badly affected. Plant in full or partial sun and space 12 to 18 inches (30 to 46 cm). These plants slowly spread, so a single established plant can become an entire patch if you divide it in autumn. I especially love the tall, sweetly scented *Phlox paniculata* varieties, including white-flowered 'David', mauve-flowered 'Laura', and the two-toned pink beauty 'Bright Eyes'. **Vase life tricks:** Harvest when just 2 or 3 florets are open on a stem, and place in water with preservative for a 5- to 7-day vase life.

PHLOX

DELPHINIUM

YARROW

YARROW The flat-topped flower heads of this drought-tolerant, airy bloomer come in a stunning range of cranberries, pinks, peaches, oranges, yellows, whites, and lavenders. Available in both single colors and mixes, they have so many options to choose from. Grow them in full sun and space the plants 18 inches (46 cm) apart. Yarrow is a vigorous spreader, so be sure to give it plenty of room to wander. My favorite varieties are peachy 'Appleblossom'; the stunning blend of raspberries, blushes, and corals in the Summer Berries Mix; rusty orange 'Terra Cotta'; and common white. **Vase life tricks:** Harvest when 80 percent of the flowers are open on a stem. It's tempting to pick them when less mature, but the young stems will wilt within just a few hours if you do. Yarrow benefits from floral preservative and will last for about a week in the vase.

ROSES

———

Few plants in the early summer garden can rival the fleeting beauty of a blossom-smothered rose bush. Harvesting their fragrant, delicate blossoms is an experience not to be missed. Roses have had me under their spell for years. Right now, I grow close to 400 rose bushes in more than 50 different varieties.

HOW TO GROW

If you peruse your local bookstore or library you will find hundreds of books about this exquisite family of plants. There is so much information to sort through that it can feel a little overwhelming if you're just starting out. Over the years, I've tried many of the remedies and tricks out there and have found that the best chance of growing healthy roses comes from focusing on three main things: giving them a sunny spot to live in; giving them rich, heavily amended soil; and choosing varieties that have strong disease resistance.

While you can buy plants in pots at your local nursery for much of the year, I order mine directly from the mail-order rose catalogs as bare-root plants in the winter. Bushes arrive dormant in late winter/early spring, and when planted right away, they generally outperform container-grown varieties. The benefit to buying bare-root stock is that they don't experience transplant shock and are available as large plants.

To plant, dig a hole twice the size of the rose's roots and gently set the plant in the hole. Take care to not bunch or squeeze the roots together in the hole; give them enough room to fully spread out. Fill the hole with amended soil, making sure to fully cover the trunk, up to the graft (the little raised scar that goes around the plant

where the root ball is attached). After planting in winter, mulch with a thick layer of wood chips or rotted leaves to keep weeds down and help conserve moisture.

In late autumn, clean up all dead leaves from around the plants and mound compost or aged manure around the base of each bush. This will help insulate the crowns from damaging cold weather.

After your roses' first year of growth, pruning them is an important task that will help them bloom and grow abundantly each year. The rule of thumb with roses is the more you cut back, the more vigorous next year's growth will be. In mild climates, this can be done in late winter, but in areas where it's colder, wait until early spring, when signs of new growth are present on the plants. Start by removing any dead or diseased wood, cutting just above an outward-facing bud. I usually aim to remove about one-third of the plant's overall growth and make sure to take off any stems that are thin or weak.

In the spring, pull back the mulch you laid in autumn and work a cup of natural fertilizer, specially formulated for roses, into the soil around their roots.

Roses are definitely more disease prone than many of the other plants listed in this book. Warm, wet weather will bring on black spot, rust, and powdery mildew. I focus on growing varieties that have strong disease resistance and work to keep them as healthy as possible by spraying them with weekly applications of compost tea, removing any sick foliage, and watering only through drip irrigation. Disease is just something that comes along with roses, but if you choose suitable varieties for your climate and baby them just a little, you'll be rewarded with buckets and buckets of blooms.

FAVORITE VARIETIES

COLETTE Blooms from this stunning climber are a sumptuous shade of peachy-apricot pink. The plant's disease-resistant foliage and free-flowering habit make it a must-have for cutting.

CROWN PRINCESS MARGARETA I have a thing for yellow roses. Of the two dozen golden varieties I grow, this one always comes out on top. It's highly productive, and the flowers are the richest shade of apricot-orange gold.

'DISTANT DRUMS' Of all the roses I've seen, none quite compares to this unusually toned beauty. The medium-sized bushes are very cold hardy and vigorous and produce a continual display of blooms all summer. As the smoky lavender buds unfurl, they reveal large flowers that are a unique mix of bronze, mauve, and pale chocolate.

'EGLANTYNE' This medium-sized, disease-resistant, continual-flowering variety has one of the most exquisite flower displays I've ever seen. Its large pale pink blooms are sweetly scented and look as if they belong in a Dutch still-life painting.

JAMES GALWAY There is something almost haunting about this particular rose—it looks like it's out of a painting from another time. The large flower sprays are smothered in blooms in a sweet blend of warm pink tones. It has a large growth habit and massive, nearly thornless stems.

'SALLY HOLMES' This outstanding continual-flowering shrub rose is loaded with large sprays of creamy white single blooms with rich golden centers all summer long. These plants are vigorous.

VASE LIFE TRICKS

Roses are quite fleeting as cut flowers, lasting only a handful of days once picked. To maximize their life in the vase, harvest when the flowers are only about a third of the way open, in the cool of the morning, and get them straight into water mixed with floral preservative. For single-petaled varieties, pick them in colored bud, before they've opened and been pollinated; otherwise, the flower centers will turn brown in the vase and their petals will drop quickly. Depending on the cultivar and stage of harvest, expect 3 to 6 days of vase life for roses.

CROWN PRINCESS MARGARETA

'DISTANT DRUMS'

COLETTE

'SALLY HOLMES'

'EGLANTYNE'

JAMES GALWAY

SNAPDRAGONS

Snapdragons have always been one of the most productive early summer bloomers in my cutting garden. They're true cut-and-come-again flowers, meaning the more you pick them, the more they will flower. Last year I grew a staggering 27 varieties, with a total of 6,000 plants. You could say I'm pretty sweet on this flower. Unlike store-bought blooms, garden-grown snapdragons also carry a sweet, citrusy scent that will fill a room with fragrance for days.

When most gardeners hear "snapdragon," they think of the cheerful little packs of bedding plants available at most garden centers and hardware stores during the spring. While these technically belong in the same family, they couldn't be further from the cut flower wonders that can be cultivated. Most of these bedding types are selected for their compact size and are often treated with growth regulators to keep them extra compact for window boxes and pots. To get the ultraproductive, long-stemmed cutting types that flower for many months each summer, it's essential that you select the proper ones and grow your own from seed.

HOW TO GROW

Snapdragon seed is some of the tiniest you'll ever see. We joke that it's more like dust than seed. It can be tempting to scatter a thick layer of it over the soil surface and call it a day, but a little extra effort is required. I start it in earliest spring. Using a slightly damp toothpick, pick up just 1 or 2 seeds and place them into a cell of your seed tray, then cover with a light dusting of vermiculite. While the seed is small, it is also mighty, and you'll see the first seedlings emerge just 4 to 5 days after sowing them.

Once plants have 3 sets of true leaves, you can transplant them out into the garden, spacing plants 9 inches (23 cm) apart. Snapdragons are quite tolerant of cold and can handle a few light frosts, so plant them about a month before your last spring frost date.

To increase the number of blooms from your plants, pinching is recommended. When plants have 5 sets of true leaves, take a pair of sharp pruners and snip off the tip, leaving just 3 sets of true leaves. This will encourage the plants to branch from the base and produce up to twice as many flowers. Because pinching delays flowering by 2 to 3 weeks, I generally pinch half of my plants and leave the other half to flower early.

Snapdragons are vigorous, upright growers and have a tendency to tip over in stormy spring weather. Shortly after pinching the plants, put a layer of flower netting about a foot (30 cm) off the ground so that, as they lengthen, they can grow up through the net for extra support.

CHANTILLY MIX

FAVORITE VARIETIES

CHANTILLY MIX This gorgeous palette of ruffled, butterfly-type blooms is one of our most requested and beloved crops of the early summer. Customers actually jump up and down clapping when the first bunches arrive. I have grown all of the colors, but over time I have narrowed my favorites to the best sellers: pink (it's actually coral), light pink, bronze, and light salmon. I often combine stems from these into one bunch, and they look like fluffy bunches of fresh fruit sherbet.

MADAME BUTTERFLY MIX Also known as azalea snapdragons, these double-petaled beauties are a rare and special treat. Because of their fullness, they are difficult for insects to pollinate, so their blooms last longer in the vase than single-flowered types. This stunning, ultraruffled mix includes ivory, cherry, pink, yellow, bronze, and peach flowers.

VASE LIFE TRICKS

Harvest snapdragons when just the bottom 2 or 3 flowers are open, before they can be pollinated by insects. You can expect 7 to 10 days of vase life if you use flower preservative in the water.

MADAME BUTTERFLY MIX

TENDER ANNUALS

Tender annuals are the true stalwarts of the summer garden. They require little care, establish rapidly, flower abundantly for an extended period of time, and can take the heat of high summer.

HOW TO GROW

Because these plants are all very cold sensitive, even the slightest nip of frost will be the end of them, so don't start seeds too early. I hold off until about 6 weeks before our last spring frost to sow them, and then do successive sowings every 3 weeks through early summer. Plant seedlings in the garden once all threat of frost has passed.

The plants listed here are vigorous growers and require room to spread out, so space plants 12 to 18 inches (30 to 46 cm) apart. While all of these do well in the heat, be sure to water deeply at least once a week.

FAVORITE VARIETIES

CELOSIA A few years ago I got bitten by the celosia bug and decided to do an exhaustive 66-variety trial to find the very best varieties for cutting. I can honestly say that all of the plants were beautiful and productive, but there were a handful that really stole my heart. What's so amazing about this group of plants is that their fuzzy, velvet-like flowers come in distinct shapes—including fans, plumes, and brains—and it's hard to believe that they are actually related. Growers in warmer parts of the world can sow seeds directly in the garden, but here, where summers are more mild, I plant as seedlings in low tunnels or the hoop house. All of the celosias except the Bombay Series

(fan) benefit greatly from pinching (see page 37). When plants are about 6 inches (15 cm) tall, just snip out the growing tips. This will encourage abundant branching from the base and reward you with dozens of perfectly sized stems from each plant. My favorite varieties are 'Bombay Pink' (fan), 'Kurume Orange Red' (brain), the Pampas Plume Mix (plume), the Supercrest Mix (a blend of brain, fan, and plume), and 'Sylphide' (plume). **Vase life tricks:** Flower heads get bigger as they grow in the ground, so pick flowers when they are the size that you want but before they go to seed. Strip 80 percent of the foliage off during harvest, since it will wilt long before the flower heads fade in the vase. Celosias are an insanely long-lasting cut flower, often persisting for up to 2 weeks without preservative. Flowers can also be dried for later use. To dry, hang freshly cut stems upside down in a warm, dark place for 2 to 3 weeks or until they are firm to the touch.

CHOCOLATE QUEEN ANNE'S LACE (*Daucus carota*) This large burgundy-chocolate-colored lace flower has been an absolute hit at the farm from day one. It looks great en masse, pairs well with almost anything, and blooms for most of the summer from just one planting. The lacy flower heads come in a range of sizes and chocolaty shades, adding a dramatic, airy quality to finished arrangements. Plants get large, so space them 18 inches (46 cm) apart, and be sure to stake them early so that they don't topple over in heavy spring rains. I recommend using flower netting attached to sturdy posts, since these plants are quite bulky. **Vase life tricks:** Pick when flowers have fully opened and are lying flat. If harvested much earlier, stems have a tendency to wilt. Fresh flowers will last for 6 to 8 days in the vase with flower preservative.

GOMPHRENA

MARIGOLD

CELOSIA

CHOCOLATE QUEEN ANNE'S LACE

GOMPHRENA This late-summer darling has adorable, buttonlike blooms that resemble vividly colored clover blossoms and look great in bouquets. They thrive in the heat, so I grow mine in the low tunnel. Plants are naturally branching, so no pinching is needed. My favorite varieties all belong to the QIS Series, including Carmine, Lilac, Orange, Pink, and White. **Vase life tricks:** The more you cut them, the more they will bloom, and freshly harvested flowers can last for up to 2 weeks in the vase without preservative. Flowers can also be dried for later use. To dry, hang freshly cut stems upside down in a warm, dark place for 2 to 3 weeks or until they are firm to the touch. Be gentle when handling them after they've been dried, because the blooms are a little fragile and can fall apart easily.

MARIGOLDS These are some of the toughest, most abundant flowering plants you can grow. I often get 15 to 20 blooms from a single plant. These garden workhorses benefit from pinching early on, when they are about 6 inches (15 cm) tall. Because the vivid orange and yellow flowers are so sturdy, they also make wonderful materials for garlands and leis. My two favorite varieties are the giant tangerine-colored 'Jedi Orange' and mahogany-and-yellow-striped 'Court Jester'. **Vase life tricks:** Harvest when flowers are about halfway open, and strip off most of the foliage on the main stem. While marigold blooms are pretty basic, they are a great addition to mixed bouquets and will last for 7 to 10 days in the vase with floral preservative.

VEGETABLES

One of my favorite things to include in any bouquet is some kind of edible ingredient, and the more recognizable the better. Over the years I've tucked carrots into a famous chef's bridal bouquet, included chili peppers and tiny eggplant in food-loving grooms' boutonnieres, sprinkled cherry tomatoes and grapes into hundreds of centerpieces, added raspberries to altar arrangements, threaded crabapples into guestbook displays, and woven scented herbs into as many floral designs as I could manage.

There's nothing quite like pairing food with flowers to get a conversation going. Most people don't pay much attention to what's in a vase unless they recognize the ingredients, and a little food is usually all it takes to get non-flower-obsessed folks talking.

HOW TO GROW

All of these vegetables love the heat and produce abundantly from late summer through the first fall frost. Because my garden is situated in an area with relatively cool summers, I grow them all in a hoop house for an added level of heat. But if your garden gets plenty of hot weather, these should thrive for you outdoors.

Start seed indoors, in trays, 6 to 10 weeks before your last spring frost date. Once seedlings have their first true set of leaves, transplant them into 4-inch (10-cm) wide pots until it's safe to plant outside. Note that it's important to keep these plants at 60° to 70°F (15° to 21°C) while young in order to keep them growing. Once the weather has warmed and stabilized, with night temps above 50°F (10°C), you can plant them outdoors. All of the vegetables I include here get quite large and need room to spread out, so space them at least 12 to 18 inches (30 to 46 cm) apart. They all benefit from staking, too. For tomatoes, I recommend heavy metal T-posts to which you can tie the plants as they grow. Peppers and eggplants can be either netted or tied to a sturdy stake about 3 feet (1 m) tall.

FAVORITE VARIETIES

EGGPLANT I love to pair the skinny purple varieties of this unique fruit with other richly colored ingredients, such as chocolate lace flower, orach, and 'Queen Red Lime' zinnias. The Asian types like 'Machiaw', 'Orient Charm', and 'Orient Express' are my favorites because their fruits are long and slender and hang over the lip of a vase beautifully. These can be a little tricky to work into arrangements because the fruit is heavy, so you really have to make sure that the stems are securely in place; if plants are left to develop into the late summer and early autumn, the stems will be long enough to get into water with the fruit still attached. If you want to use them earlier in the season before the stems lengthen, you can lay the eggplant in little piles at the base of flower-filled vases. **Vase life tricks:** Take extra care when handling, since the fruit pops off the stem pretty easily. Once cut, remove all of the foliage so that the fruit is exposed. They will persist for a number of days in an arrangement.

PEPPERS Like the other vegetables, there are many varieties to choose from, and in addition to using them in summer bouquets, I love to incorporate them into fall wreaths and swags for an added level of intrigue. While most can be used with success, I prefer those with long, thin fruit, including 'Bangkok', 'Cheyenne', and 'Hungarian Hot Wax'. **Vase life tricks:** Peppers can be harvested at any stage from green all the way to full color. Handling the stems with bare hands can often leave your fingers tingling, so wear gloves when picking, and remove all of the foliage right

away, since it will wilt. Stems will persist for 2 to 3 weeks in the vase, with or without preservative.

TOMATOES Probably my all-time favorite vegetables to sneak into bouquets, tomatoes look amazing tumbling over the edge of any size arrangement. While all tomatoes can technically be used as floral design ingredients, I especially love the smaller-fruited types like 'Red Currant' and 'White Currant', since they are the easiest to incorporate. For larger arrangements, the shiny black-purple-red fruits of 'Indigo Cherry Drops' and 'Yellow Pear' look amazing. **Vase life**

tricks: Harvest after all of the fruit has developed on a cluster, but before they completely develop their mature color, since that's when they begin to loosen from the stems. Then remove all of the leaves, as they will wilt. Once ripe, the fruit has a tendency to fall from the stem, so be sure to pick them early. If attached to a stem that's in water, the fruit will persist for 4 to 5 days and change color as it ripens.

TOMATOES

PEPPERS   EGGPLANT

ZINNIAS

Nothing says summer more than an armload of cheerful zinnias. Available in a riot of brilliant colors, these happy blooms are a must-grow for any flower gardener. As one of the easiest cut flowers to cultivate, zinnias are a perfect first crop for beginning growers and are reliable, prolific producers no matter where you garden. I've been growing zinnias since the beginning, and every year I fall more and more in love with them.

HOW TO GROW

Zinnias resent cold weather and prefer to be planted after things have warmed up a bit. I know many growers in warmer parts of the world who successfully plant zinnias from seed directly in the soil, 2 or 3 weeks after their last frost. Here in cool Washington, we start our plants inside 4 to 6 weeks before setting them outside. We sow seeds in trays in the greenhouse and plant them out 2 to 3 weeks after our last frost date.

Space plants 1 foot (30 cm) apart. Sow successive crops of zinnias every 2 to 3 weeks through early summer in order to have a steady stream of these beautiful blooms for bouquets through autumn. (See page 24 to learn about succession planting.)

Be sure to choose tall cutting varieties, such as my favorites listed here, and grow them in full sun. After the baby plants are snuggled into their permanent homes, water weekly, by drip or soaker hose, for at least half an hour or until the ground is deeply soaked.

The secret to growing long-stemmed zinnias is pinching. When plants are about 18 inches (46 cm) tall, snip out the center flower bud. This will encourage plants to develop branches low on the plant and ultimately produce longer stems. If you are not regularly harvesting your zinnias, be sure to deadhead any spent blooms to help direct the plant's energy into producing new flowers.

FAVORITE VARIETIES

BENARY'S GIANT SERIES The largest-flowered variety in the zinnia family, these plants often reach 4 to 5 feet (120 to 152 cm) and have a high percentage of double flowers. They come in a bright color range with strong stems and good disease resistance. My favorite colors are Salmon Rose, Coral, Orange, and Giant Wine.

'OKLAHOMA SALMON' This gorgeous bloomer is one of the most prolific zinnias I've ever grown. Its petite, double flowers are a warm mix of salmon and peach, and they look good when combined with almost anything. The long, strong stems and small flower size make them a winning summer crop and wonderful bouquet addition.

QUEEN SERIES This series features long stems, lasting vase life, and good disease resistance. There are two colors in this series: 'Queen Lime' is a beautiful Granny Smith apple green with medium-sized flower heads atop strong, sturdy stems, and 'Queen Red Lime' is a gorgeous novelty flower sought out for its unique coloring, a mash-up of eggplant, green, and rose.

SCABIOSA FLOWERED MIX The first time I grew these, they became one of my favorite new crops. The frilly double blooms look like mini gerbera daisies or double-flowered echinaceas. They have long stems and come in a sherbet-toned mix, ranging from scarlet to gold to orange.

BENARY'S GIANT SERIES

'OKLAHOMA SALMON'

178

QUEEN SERIES

'UPROAR ROSE'

SCABIOSA FLOWERED MIX

SUNBOW MIX

SUNBOW MIX These adorable little darlings stole my heart when I trialed them. Their miniature 1- to 2-inch (2- to 5-cm) double blooms open atop long, sturdy stems and come in a cheery palette of gold, scarlet, orange, pink, white, rose, and purple.

'UPROAR ROSE' This variety is a true cutting garden workhorse. It has super long stems and great disease resistance, and is one of the most productive zinnias I've ever grown. The flowers are an electric magenta pink, well loved by our customers and gorgeous in mixed bouquets.

VASE LIFE TRICKS

To tell whether a zinnia is ready to harvest, grab the stem about 8 inches (20 cm) down from the flower and gently shake the stem. If the stem is droopy or bends much at all, it is not quite ready to cut. If the stem is stiff and remains erect, it is ready to harvest. If floral preservative is added to the water, zinnias should last for 7 to 10 days in the vase.

Summer
Projects

DAHLIAS EN MASSE

Of all of the flowers I've ever grown, few have made as lasting an impression as the 'Café au Lait' dahlia. While one gigantic blossom is incredible, a vase overflowing with dozens of these beauties is showstopping. The massive flower heads and creamy, blush-tinted, silklike petals are a sight to behold. It's no surprise that dahlias are one of the most requested blooms for summer weddings.

Because they are so large, weaving these flowers into arrangements can be a little tricky. My solution is to simply let them steal the show and display them en masse alongside subtle companions. This arrangement is substantial—about 3 feet (91 cm) tall and wide—which is the perfect way to showcase these breathtaking blooms. For this arrangement, it's essential to choose a stable crock or vase that won't tip over when filled with top-heavy stems.

YOU WILL NEED

A large crock or heavy vase

A ball of chicken wire

Eight 2- to 3-foot (0.6- to 1-m) long branches of fruited crabapples

Fifteen 2- to 3-foot (0.6- to 1-m) long stems of green ninebark foliage

Six 2- to 3-foot (0.6- to 1-m) long stems of ninebark with seed heads

25 'Café au Lait' dahlias

6 stems of 'Appleblossom' dahlias

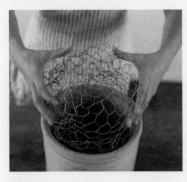

1 Start by filling your vase to the brim with water mixed with floral preservative. Compress a piece of chicken wire into a ball and push down into the vase to help anchor the weighty blossoms and branches that would otherwise topple out.

2 Remove the foliage from the crabapple branches so that the fruit is more visible, then place the crabapple branches evenly around the lip of the vase. Make sure that the stems are securely in place so that they don't fall out.

3 Place the ninebark foliage stems so that they're arching in the same way as the crabapple branches, making sure you don't cover up the crabapples.

4 Use the ninebark seed head stems to fill in between the other foliage ingredients. These will add a light, airy quality to the finished arrangement.

5 Add the dahlias. Dinner plate–sized types, like 'Café au Lait', are very top-heavy, and the petals bruise quite easily, so take your time and be gentle when handling them. Starting around the edges of the vase, place the most arching stems first so that they look like they are spilling over the edges. Then fill in the center of the bouquet. For a more natural look, cut flowers at different heights, giving each one room to shine, and place some facing at an angle and toward the back. All sides of this flower are beautiful.

6 Tuck the stems of smaller, complementary-colored, single-petaled 'Appleblossom' dahlias among the larger blooms.

7 Stand back and take a look at the arrangement. Fill in any holes or empty spots with more ninebark foliage or stems with seed heads.

SUMMER SUNSET BOUQUET

High summer equals supreme abundance in the garden, and I try my best to savor the bounty by displaying a bouquet in every room of the house. Nothing brings me more into the moment than fresh flowers straight from the garden. I have mentioned that I love combining vegetables and flowers in bouquets. There are many wonderful foodie options that look beautiful in the vase, including herbs, tiny tomatoes on the vine, unripe fruit on the branch, baby eggplant, and even beans and peas. Visitors always comment whenever I incorporate these ingredients into an arrangement— edible-infused bouquets are definite conversation starters.

I am in love with the bright, shaggy dahlia called 'Punkin Spice'; its casual form and warm harvest color make it a perfect choice for this dazzling bouquet. For the button dahlias, the adorable, soft orange 'Amber Queen' is a longtime favorite. The airy plumed celosias are perfect for filling in any holes or gaps, and Lemon basil brings a lovely citrusy scent to any room it's in.

YOU WILL NEED

A flower frog

A medium pitcher

5 stems of raspberry foliage

2 clusters of cherry tomatoes on the vine

7 stems of Lemon basil

5 stems of medium-sized dahlias, such as 'Punkin Spice'

7 stems of small button dahlias, such as 'Amber Queen'

5 stems of plumed celosia

4 stems of petite zinnias, such as 'Oklahoma Salmon'

5 stems of gomphrena

1 Place the flower frog in the pitcher, and fill with water and floral preservative. This will help anchor the heavier stems.

2 Establish the overall shape of the arrangement by placing raspberry greens around the edge of the pitcher.

3 Place the cherry tomato clusters at the front of the arrangement, tumbling over the edge, so that they really stand out.

4 Add the Lemon basil, spacing the stems evenly throughout the bouquet.

5 Start placing the flowers. The medium-sized dahlias are the stars of the bouquet, so be sure to face them forward and around the edge of the vase so they're not hidden by the foliage.

6 Tuck in the complementary-colored button dahlias among the larger blooms.

7 Weave the celosias in among the other flowers.

8 Poke in the zinnias, making sure that they are a bit higher than the other blooms so they don't get lost among the other elements.

9 Weave in the gomphrena anywhere that needs a little pop of color.

HAND-TIED MARKET BOUQUET

One of the best parts of growing a cutting garden is having enough bounty to share. I absolutely love taking a quick stroll through my flower beds, gathering an armload of blooms, and whipping together a quick gift bouquet for a family member or friend.

The simplest way to create a cheery bouquet that looks like what you might see at the farmers market is by loosely following the European spiral technique. This involves holding the bouquet in your hand as you add flowers and foliage, at a slight angle, while rotating the arrangement to produce an abundant-looking display that makes the perfect fresh-from-the-garden present.

YOU WILL NEED

Pruners

Sisal twine

4 stems of lavender delphinium

5 stems of purple basil

5 to 7 stems of chocolate Queen Anne's lace

6 stems of pink double-flowered cosmos such as Double Click

8 to 10 stems of purple small-flowered zinnias, such as 'Sunbow'

5 stems of purple gomphrena, such as QIS

6 to 8 stems of large-flowered zinnias, such as 'Queen Red Lime'

2 stems of scented geraniums

1 Remove the foliage from the lower two-thirds of each stem. Then lay the flowers out in little piles by type on a worktable, flower heads facing away from you.

2 To create the spiraled look you're after, build the bouquet while holding it in your hand. With the exception of the first stem, which will ultimately be at the center, add stems at an angle of about 25 degrees evenly around the bouquet, and turn the bouquet slightly as you add blooms for overall balance. As a general guide, for every complete 360-degree turn of the bouquet, I probably add 5 or 6 stems while rotating the bunch.

3 Start with a long stem of delphinium and add the basil stems as you turn the bouquet.

4 After each basil stem, tuck in a chocolate Queen Anne's lace, then thread in a cosmos, continuing to slightly rotate the bunch as you add each new stem.

5 Add the small-flowered zinnias, spacing them evenly around the bouquet, remembering to add the blooms at an angle.

6 Nestle the remaining delphinium stems around the arrangement.

7 From above, insert the cute little gomphrena blooms throughout the bouquet, making sure that they poke up above the other flowers so they really stand out.

8 Place the large-flowered zinnias around the bouquet, spacing them as evenly as possible.

9 Add the scented geranium stems around the edge to infuse the bouquet with fragrance.

10 Cut the bottom of the stems so that they're all the same length.

11 Lay the bouquet on the table. While holding everything together with one hand, wrap a piece of twine around the stems a few times, and tie the twine with a simple knot.

AUT

COMPLETING THE HARVEST
&
PUTTING THE
GARDEN TO BED

Autumn always has a funny way of sneaking up on me. One day I'm blissfully immersed in summer's abundance, trying my best to stay on top of it all, and then, without a speck of warning, everything changes overnight. The days suddenly get shorter, the late afternoon shadows grow longer, and on early mornings in the garden I need an extra layer of clothing just to stay comfortable. The plants are no longer putting their energy into growth, but are instead racing to set seed before the first frost arrives. The once rich, sparkling green field quickly shifts to a dull, warm gold, and within just a few short weeks the landscape is nearly unrecognizable.

But while most of the garden is quickly fading, a few plants carry us through the season. The dahlias bloom abundantly until the first hard frost. As the foliage canopy in the pumpkin and squash patch withers away, the brilliant, textural green, white, orange, and golden fruits are finally revealed. The chrysanthemums come into their own and produce a staggering amount of flowers, in dozens of colors and shapes, over a 6-week stretch of time.

As autumn progresses, my focus shifts from growing and tending to cleaning up and putting the garden to bed. There is work to be done, but unlike spring and summer, the level of urgency disappears, and I can take my time with each project.

Autumn
Tasks

TAKE NOTES

Record keeping is important, and I always set aside some time in early autumn to jot down notes before the frost wipes away all evidence of that year's garden. I document what worked, what didn't, and what I want to change for the coming year. It's tempting to skip this step, thinking I'll remember all of the little details many months later, but good notes are key to planning and having more success the following year.

CLEAN UP

One of the biggest and most daunting chores of the entire year is tidying up and putting the garden to bed in autumn. I always find it hard to get started, never really knowing where to begin. It's easy to procrastinate, but I've found that it's best to just jump in and tackle this task shortly after the first autumn frost. You never know what kind of weather is on the horizon this time of year, and it's really a relief to get all of the old plants pulled out and the irrigation and fabric removed and stored before the weather gets bad.

DIG DAHLIAS

Dahlias are very cold sensitive, and in all but the warmest areas they will die if left in the ground over the winter. While it's generally safe to postpone digging through late autumn to early winter, as long as the ground doesn't freeze solid, I like to err on the side of caution and get them out of the soil as soon as a stretch of sunny days arrives after a few fall frosts. Once dug, the tubers must be stored in a spot that won't drop below freezing, such as an insulated garage or a basement. (See page 135 for more details on digging up, dividing, and storing dahlias.)

PULL UP AND BRING IN TENDER PERENNIALS

There are a handful of perennials that won't survive the cold temperatures of winter unless they are brought indoors and stored somewhere that stays above freezing. Both chrysanthemums and scented geraniums fall into this category. Because I grow both of these plants inside a hoop house, they stay in production for quite a while after the rest of the garden has been taken down by frost. After they've finished producing and before a hard frost hits and the ground starts to freeze,

I cut back these plants so only 6 inches (15 cm) of foliage remains, dig them up, and store them in soil-filled pots in a frost-free place such as a basement, garage, or minimally heated greenhouse.

PLANT HARDY ANNUAL SEEDS IN THE GROUND

It always feels a little strange to plant seeds in the autumn, but for a handful of super-hardy annuals, this is the ideal time to get them in the ground for an earlier spring bloom. In really cold climates, larkspur and love-in-a-mist can be sown directly in the ground and will make it through the winter unscathed. In more temperate climates, false Queen Anne's lace, bells of Ireland, orach, and cerinthe can be added to the autumn planting list (where it's colder, plant these in late winter in seed trays indoors and then transplant into the garden in the spring). I aim to get seed in the ground shortly after the first frost. These seeds benefit from the freeze-thaw-freeze cycle of early autumn, and they will generally sprout 10 to 14 days after planting. They will form low clumps of foliage that will overwinter and send up abundant flower spikes in spring.

SOW SWEET PEAS

In mild climates, sweet peas can be sown in pots in early autumn and then overwintered in a hoop house or cold frame, to be planted into the garden in early spring. This approach produces bushier plants that will start flowering up to 6 weeks sooner than those from seeds sown in late winter to early spring. But note that while sweet peas can take some cold, they must be protected from temperatures much below freezing or they will become stressed or die.

PLANT SPRING-FLOWERING BULBS

This is one of my favorite autumn tasks. There is so much promise and hope in each little bulb, and they always get me so excited about the year to come. It's important to plant them before the ground starts to freeze very deeply so that they have a chance to form roots and get established before their growth is halted by the cold. I aim for planting no later than a month after the first autumn frost.

POT UP PAPERWHITES AND AMARYLLISES

In addition to filling the garden with bulbs that will bloom abundantly during the early spring months, it's important to plan ahead for the long months of winter. I set aside a corner of my garage to hold a big collection of pots planted with winter-flowering bulbs such as paperwhites and amaryllises. I plant them shortly after I get the garden put to bed, then bring in a half dozen pots every few weeks for a continuous display of fragrance and color in the house all winter long.

PLANT PERENNIALS AND SHRUBS

One of the best times to plant perennials and shrubs, both evergreen and deciduous, is in autumn. You ideally want to get them into the ground at least 6 weeks before the soil freezes deeply and temperatures plummet, so aim for early to midseason. Once they are planted, I mulch them deeply, both to help protect roots from temperature extremes and to minimize weeds. I give perennials a 2- to 4-inch (5- to 10-cm) top dressing of aged compost and shrubs a 4- to 6-inch (10- to 15-cm) layer of wood chips.

TEST AND AMEND SOIL

Autumn is the best time to take a soil sample and apply the recommended amendments like lime and trace minerals. This gives the nutrients time to blend into the soil so that any deficiencies will be remedied and the next year's garden will be healthier. See "Perform a Soil Test" (page 20) and "Feed Your Soil" (page 27) for more details.

Autumn Blooms,
Edibles &
Textural Stems

BLACK-EYED SUSANS

Black-eyed Susans (*Rudbeckia*) are hardworking plants that should be included in every cutting garden. They are heat tolerant and low maintenance, and they flower steadily and abundantly for many months from mid-summer through early autumn. While they bloom most profusely in summer, I think they look best in autumn. Mixing these harvest-hued bloomers with grains, grasses, and sunflowers always makes a winning combination.

This group of plants is massive and filled with so many choices that it can be hard to rein yourself in. But when it comes to varieties best suited for cutting, I suggest sticking with the taller *Rudbeckia hirta* and the wildly abundant *Rudbeckia triloba*. They will bless you with buckets and buckets of blooms over the longest period of time, and while technically considered perennials, both do best when sown early and grown as annuals.

HOW TO GROW

Start seed indoors in trays 8 to 10 weeks before your last spring frost and transplant out after all danger of frost has passed. Plants get quite bushy, so give them at least 12 inches (30 cm) of space in a sunny spot to spread out. All of the varieties listed here grow tall and have a tendency to topple over in full bloom without proper support. I recommend either netting or corralling them early on for best results.

FAVORITE VARIETIES

RUDBECKIA HIRTA CHEROKEE SUNSET MIX

One of the tallest varieties for cutting, this mix is filled with large, double-flowered types in rust, bronze, gold, chocolate, and many eye-catching bicolor flowers. This palette is the epitome of autumn.

RUDBECKIA HIRTA 'CHERRY BRANDY'

A breakthrough introduction, this beauty is the first-ever red variety available from seed. Its deep maroon red petals surround a dark chocolate center and look incredible when combined with other moody plant materials, such as 'Queen Red Lime' zinnias and 'Aromato' basil.

RUDBECKIA HIRTA CHIM CHIMINEE MIX

This rust-toned mix is one of my favorite late summer/early autumn bloomers. The large flower heads and fuzzy quilled petals are striking in shades of chocolate, bronze, rust red, gold, and burnt orange. I love pairing this variety with dark sunflowers and ninebark foliage.

RUDBECKIA HIRTA 'DENVER DAISY'

This eye-catching variety boasts large golden yellow blooms with dark chocolaty red centers that look almost like they've been hand painted. No two are exactly the same, and the unique coloring makes these beauties a must-have.

RUDBECKIA HIRTA CHEROKEE
SUNSET MIX

RUDBECKIA HIRTA 'CHERRY BRANDY'

RUDBECKIA HIRTA CHIM CHIMINEE MIX

RUDBECKIA HIRTA 'DENVER DAISY'

RUDBECKIA HIRTA 'PRAIRIE SUN'

RUDBECKIA TRILOBA

RUDBECKIA HIRTA 'INDIAN SUMMER'

RUDBECKIA HIRTA 'INDIAN SUMMER' One of the largest flowering varieties, this semi-double monster produces blooms that range from 4 to 7 inches (10 to 18 cm) across. The school bus yellow petals are beautifully accented with the clear black eye.

RUDBECKIA HIRTA 'PRAIRIE SUN' This tall, freely blooming variety is always a favorite bouquet addition. Its bicolor petals are a cheerful mix of dark and light yellow that radiate around the pretty apple green center.

RUDBECKIA TRILOBA Of all of the black-eyed Susans I've ever grown, this is my absolute favorite. By midsummer, this variety can easily reach a towering 5 to 6 feet (1.6 to 2 m) tall, with individual plants producing up to 20 stems each! The miniature-sized flowers are borne in airy sprays, and when added to arrangements, they bring a happy, uplifting quality.

VASE LIFE TRICKS

Harvest black-eyed Susans when flowers are beginning to open, and you can expect a 7- to 10-day vase life if floral preservative is used. Black-eyed Susans are considered a "dirty flower" and are notorious for making their water murky within a matter of hours. To combat this and extend their vase life considerably, add a few drops of bleach to the water.

CABBAGES
AND KALES

As autumn progresses and the weather turns wet, cold, and frosty, few flowers still look good in the garden. But this is when ornamental cabbages and kales are at their finest, and tucking a tiny patch of these late-season workhorses into the garden will allow you to continue making arrangements long after most floral ingredients have faded. I love to combine the deeply crinkled leaves of kale with chrysanthemums, rose hips, and dried pods in a vase, and wire the roselike blooms of ornamental cabbages into autumn-inspired wreaths.

HOW TO GROW

Start seed in trays indoors in midsummer, about 3 months before the first autumn frost. Transplant out into the garden in a sunny spot once plants have 2 sets of true leaves (see "Starting Seeds 101" on page 31). Kales grow quite large, so give plants 12 to 18 inches (30 to 46 cm) to spread out. Ornamental cabbages require an opposite approach: to encourage smaller, more usable stems, they need be tightly crowded into planting beds, just 4 to 6 inches (10 to 15 cm) apart.

For ornamental cabbages, netting them early is essential in order to produce straight stems and keep plants from tipping over. As the plants lengthen, it's also important to periodically remove their lower leaves, which makes insect control easier. Kale plants don't need any special care.

Ornamental cabbages are prone to aphid damage. If an infestation is severe, spray weekly with insecticidal soap (in the United States, I prefer the Safer brand) until the aphids have disappeared. If caterpillars are an issue for either crop, apply Bt (*Bacillus thuringiensis*), following the directions on the bottle. Both of these treatments are organic and are safe for pets and children.

FAVORITE VARIETIES

CRANE SERIES ORNAMENTAL CABBAGE
In recent years, many new cabbage varieties have been bred for the commercial cut flower trade. I've grown nearly all of them and have found that the consistent growth habit and lovely color variations in this series make it my very favorite, and their color develops as the weather cools. 'Crane Red' has blue-green leaves and a bright purple center, 'Crane Rose' has blue-purple leaves and a bright purple center, 'Crane Feather Queen Red' has frilly purple leaves, and 'Crane White' starts out green and becomes creamy as it develops.

'REDBOR' KALE This dark purple, frilly-leaved variety is a beautiful (and delicious) addition to the garden, producing enough for meals and to be the base for many late-season bouquets. The bold leaf color is enhanced by cold weather.

'WINTERBOR' KALE An old garden standby, this blue-green, ruffled variety pairs well with just about anything and is the base of most of my late-autumn bouquets. It's also edible.

VASE LIFE TRICKS

Harvest kales when the leaves are large and firm, and remove the foliage from the lower third of the stems. Pick cabbages anytime after they take the shape of rose blossoms, and remove any remaining lower leaves. Both cabbages and kales last extremely well in the vase, up to 2 weeks, but they will make the water smell skunky after just a few days. Using floral preservative helps with this, but I recommend changing the water every few days.

'CRANE RED'

'CRANE WHITE'

'CRANE WHITE'

'CRANE FEATHER
QUEEN RED'

'REDBOR' KALE

'CRANE WHITE'

'CRANE ROSE'

'CRANE WHITE'

'WINTERBOR' KALE

CHRYSANTHEMUMS

During my first few years of professional flower growing, I heard customers speak only negatively about chrysanthemums. Synonymous with poor taste and dated floral design, cheap bunches of mums were available everywhere, and no one with an ounce of class would ever consider using them.

Like so many flowers, the chrysanthemum had fallen prey to modernization, intensive breeding, and ultimately the loss of everything that made this plant group so special. I, too, had a very low opinion of chrysanthemums—until I visited an urban flower farm in Philadelphia where the owner was cultivating the most amazing patch of heirloom mum varieties, unlike anything I'd ever seen. Their huge billowy blossoms, unique quill-shaped petals, and soft muted colors were a delightful departure from the standard mum fare I was used to. Never in my wildest dreams would I have associated such beauty and uniqueness with a chrysanthemum.

Little did I know that tucked away in backyards and flower farms and on patios and terraces around the world, the old chrysanthemum breeds were being kept alive by passionate people. Once I discovered the hidden magic of this plant family, I devoted an entire greenhouse to growing every variety I could get my hands on, and I have been singing their praises ever since.

HOW TO GROW

Chrysanthemums aren't winter hardy, so order new rooted cuttings each spring. It's best to have the plants arrive 5 to 6 weeks before the last spring frost; pot them up into 4-inch (10-cm) pots and leave them in a bright, protected spot such as a greenhouse so that they will be stocky by the time you plant them in the ground after the last frost.

There are numerous cultivars to choose from; some bloom as early as the end of summer, others shortly before winter arrives. While these plants can take a few light frosts, it's best to give them extra protection. I plant my mums in an unheated hoop house, but growers with limited space can plant them in large pots that can be moved to a sheltered spot, such as a covered porch, when you expect a hard frost.

These plants get quite large, so it's important to give them 12 to 18 inches (30 to 46 cm) of space in a sunny area and provide a strong support system from the start. If you're growing only a few plants, then a sturdy post pounded in at the base of each plant to tie it to as it grows should be adequate. I grow hundreds of plants, so for ease, I use flower netting attached to heavy metal T-posts to keep the rampant growth corralled. (See "Staking" on page 37 for detailed instructions.)

In early summer, cut back plants hard, to just 6 to 8 inches (15 to 20 cm) tall. This encourages vigorous branching from the base and will increase flower production exponentially. If you read up on mum growing, there are a number of other techniques that enthusiasts use, but I've found that plants are plenty productive if you simply cut them back at the very beginning of summer.

Mums are prone to aphids in the autumn. If the infestation is severe, spray weekly with insecticidal soap (in the United States, I prefer the Safer brand) until the aphids have disappeared. Sometimes caterpillars are an issue, too—as with cabbages, you can combat them with Bt.

'BRONZE FLEECE'

'CANDID'

FAVORITE VARIETIES

'BRONZE FLEECE' I adore this wildly productive, small anemone-flowered variety. Each stem is smothered with dozens of miniature, fuzzy, pumpkin-hued blooms that look great combined with other fall-toned flowers.

'CANDID' The finest red variety I've ever grown, this deep ruby beauty reliably produces an abundance of large flower sprays, perfect for arranging.

'HEATHER JAMES' This massive stunner produces more stems than any other variety I've grown. The thick rusty blooms have the most stunning textural quality and last for up to 2 weeks in the vase.

'JUDITH BAKER' The first time I saw this airy, deep bronze wonder, I stopped dead in my tracks. Its palm-sized flowers are a stunning blend of rich copper and warm gold, and it mixes incredibly well with other autumn treasures. I also love to display it en masse.

'NIJIN BIGO' The blond undersides of this incurve variety are a striking contrast against the orange red of the petals' inner side. The color combination makes this stocky grower a must-have for autumn.

'SEATON'S TOFFEE' This variety is the epitome of autumn, with large, deep bronze blooms, sturdy stems, and intriguing tubular florets.

VASE LIFE TRICKS

Cut stems when the flowers are one-half to two-thirds of the way open, then remove any foliage that will fall below the waterline in your vase. Chrysanthemums last an extremely long time in the vase, often more than 2 weeks with floral preservative.

'HEATHER JAMES'

'JUDITH BAKER'

'NIJIN BIGO'

'SEATON'S TOFFEE'

FRUITING BRANCHES

One treat of the autumn months that I look forward to most is having an abundance of fruiting branches to use in bouquets. The heavy, berry-laden stems add such an interesting textural quality that it's impossible not to tuck them into just about every arrangement I create.

HOW TO GROW

The following shrubs and vines are easy to grow and thrive in most climates. Choose a freely draining spot in full sun, making sure to give the plants at least 6 feet (2 m) to stretch out as they grow. The best time to plant is during the autumn or early spring if you're putting in potted plants, and winter if you're purchasing bare-root shrubs.

FAVORITE VARIETIES

BITTERSWEET This extremely vigorous vine bears long, rambling stems loaded with yellow buds that burst open to reveal bright orange fruits in the autumn. Because of their rampant growth, bittersweet is considered a noxious weed in some places, so research your state or local restrictions and take care when planting it. Provide the vines with sturdy trellising. Bittersweet needs a pollinator in order to set fruit; grow one male plant for every ten females (ask your local nursery about this if you're unsure). Fruit develops on last year's growth, so don't prune too heavily. **Vase life tricks:** Harvest before the fruit pods have popped open, when they are still greenish yellow, and remove all of the foliage. Stems can be used fresh and then left to dry either in the vase or in a warm, dry place. Dried stems can last for many years if carefully handled.

GRAPES By tucking a few of these vines around your property, you will be rewarded with basket-loads of fruit both for eating and to weave into bouquets from late summer through autumn. As the weather turns cold, the large maple-shaped leaves transform from green to gold to a marbled red-orange before dropping. After the foliage and fruit have disappeared, the remaining flexible woody stems can be cut and coiled into circles, making the perfect base for wreaths. Plant in early spring and give them a sturdy trellis to climb on. A happy grapevine can live for up to 30 years. **Vase life tricks:** Harvest fruit before it's fully ripe; otherwise, the individual grapes will fall off the stems and make a mess. Try to find clusters attached to longer branches so that they can be easily added to an arrangement (though shorter stems work well in low, short bouquets). If picked green, fruit will last for 4 to 5 days in the vase. Grape foliage, with its brilliant changing colors, also works well in the vase. Harvest anytime after the leaves begin to color up, and combine it with other autumn treasures like chrysanthemums, rose hips, and ornamental cabbages.

HYPERICUM During late summer and early autumn, this low-maintenance shrubby perennial is loaded with an abundance of shiny, brightly colored berries in shades of red, orange, pink, peach, brown, yellow, and white, depending on the variety. Plants grow quickly, and because they produce fruit on 1-year-old growth, you can have berries the first growing season if planted in spring. Space plants 18 to 24 inches (45 to 60 cm) apart. I love the dark foliaged variety 'Albury Purple' and the orange-cherry–colored 'Orange Flair'. **Vase life tricks:** Harvest when fruit begins to turn color. Stems will last for up to 2 weeks in the vase; no preservative is needed.

ROSE HIP Although harvesting these thorny treasures always involves some pain, no matter how careful I am, I think few things are more beautiful than large swollen rose hips. In addition to cultivating hundreds of repeat-flowering roses for their fragrant, fluffy blossoms, I grow a bumper crop of rose hips in the autumn. *Rosa dupontii*, a 6-foot (2-m) tall giant, bears single, creamy pink-tinged blossoms, followed by hundreds of small, elongated orange hips. After flowers fade, the blue-purple-leaved *Rosa glauca* bears heavy clusters of unique milk chocolate–colored hips that slowly change to orangey-red. And the hardy, disease-resistant, repeat-flowering *Rosa rugosa* types produce the most exquisite green, orange, and red, tomato-shaped hips when petals drop. **Vase life tricks:** Pick stems of hips while still full and before they start to shrivel, and remove all the leaves. The stems will last for a week or more in the vase without floral preservative.

SNOWBERRY Native to the United States, but available globally, these easy-to-grow shrubs are prized for their pink and white berry–loaded stems that ripen in the autumn. These plants thrive in sun or part shade and spread quickly through underground rhizomes. Because they produce fruit on 1-year-old growth, berries will develop the first autumn if planted in spring. Space plants 2 to 3 feet (60 to 91 cm) apart. Of the numerous varieties to choose from, I particularly love 'Amethyst', a large purple-pink fruited beauty that is disease resistant and produces a bumper crop of long, arching stems. **Vase life tricks:** Pick berried stems while berries are plump and before they start to shrivel, and remove the lower leaves. The stems will last for a week in the vase without floral preservative.

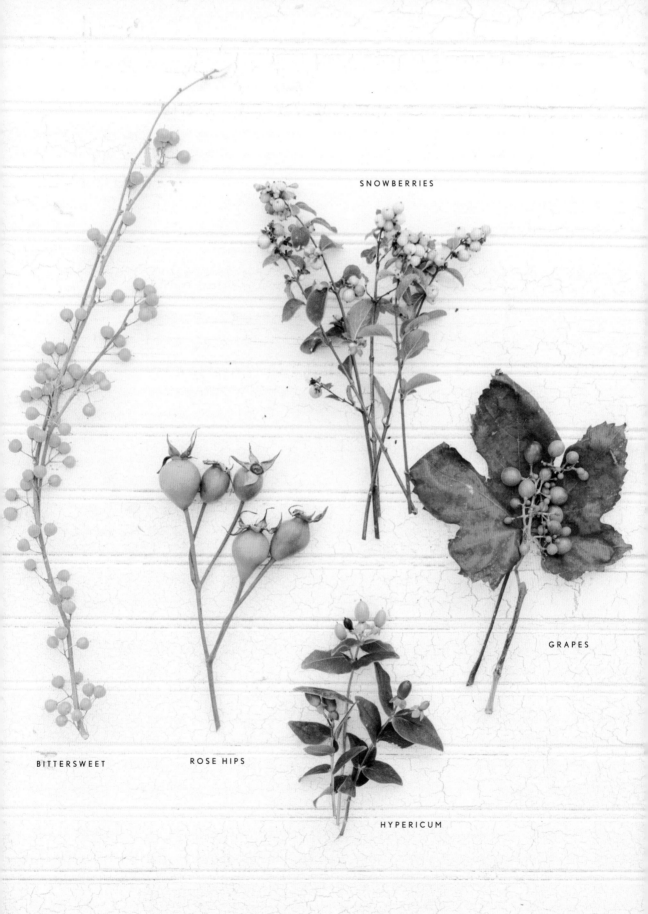

SNOWBERRIES

GRAPES

BITTERSWEET

ROSE HIPS

HYPERICUM

CRESS

AMARANTH

FLAX

GRAINS
& PODS

While I adore growing lush, romantic blooms, there's also something very satisfying about cultivating weedier, wilder bouquet ingredients. These unique textural elements add interest and depth to any arrangement with their rustic, end-of-season appeal. They produce an abundance of cutting material from midsummer through autumn.

FAVORITE VARIETIES

AMARANTH I have grown just about every variety of amaranth on the market, but I've found only a handful to be worthy of planting en masse every year. The hanging green 'Emerald Tassles' is a bouquet staple and looks smashing in large arrangements because it's super dramatic. 'Opopeo' is my favorite upright dark crimson variety, and it ripens faster than the others. 'Hot Biscuits' is an incredible golden brown that is stunning in autumn bouquets. 'Coral Fountain' is a beautiful hanging pink variety that looks like faded, crushed velvet. **How to grow:** Start seed indoors in trays 4 to 6 weeks before the last spring frost, and transplant out after all danger of frost has passed. Amaranth can also be direct seeded in the garden once all danger of frost has passed. Plant these 12 inches (30 cm) apart, and give them a hard pinch (see "Pinching," page 37) when they are 8 to 10 inches (20 to 25 cm) tall to encourage branching and a more usable stem size. **Vase life tricks:** Harvest when the seed heads get large and intensely colored. Remove most of the foliage to prevent wilting and to expose the textural blooms. You can expect a vase life of 7 to 10 days if you use floral preservative.

CRESS (*Lepidium sativum* 'Wrinkled Crinkled') This fast-flowering filler is a must-have for mixed bouquets and intricate handiwork such as boutonnieres and flower crowns. The tall, sturdy stems are smothered in beautiful silvery seedpods that aren't prone to wilting or shattering. Producing a bumper crop in just 2 months from sowing, this garden workhorse is a winner. **How to grow:** Cress is extremely quick to germinate, so I direct seed it in the garden every 2 to 3 weeks from my last spring frost through early summer for a steady supply. **Vase life tricks:** Harvest when the seedpods are fully formed and the top blooms have faded for a 7- to 10-day vase life. Besides using in a fresh arrangement, stems are easy to dry and make a fantastic addition to autumn bouquets and wreaths. To dry, hang upside down in a warm, dry place out of direct sunlight for a few weeks or until dry to the touch.

FLAX (*Linum usitatissimum*) I've been growing this treasure for many years, and I'm still as head-over-heels in love with it as the day I discovered it in a friend's garden. Its delicate seedy wands add a glittery sparkle to bouquets, and they look stunning when paired with sunflowers. **How to grow:** Start seed indoors 4 weeks before the last spring frost, and transplant out after all danger of frost has passed. For an uninterrupted harvest, sow a new batch every 2 to 3 weeks through midsummer. Space plants 2 to 4 inches (5 to 10 cm) apart. **Vase life tricks:** You can cut flax just after the flowers drop their petals and leave behind their green seedpods. These will last for up to 10 days in the vase, no preservative needed. If you are unable to harvest the entire patch in the green stage, you can pick stems and dry them as they turn golden for fall arrangements. To dry, hang upside down in a warm, dry place out of direct sunlight for a few weeks or until dry to the touch.

ORNAMENTAL GRASSES

One of the fastest and easiest ways to add unexpected magic to an arrangement is by tucking a few stems of ornamental grasses into the mix. In addition to bringing unique visual interest to bouquets, these grasses are drought tolerant, easy to grow, and bloom for months from just one planting.

FAVORITE VARIETIES

FIBER OPTIC GRASS (*Panicum elegans* 'Frosted Explosion') This is one of the most productive varieties I've ever grown. It cranks out loads of stems every few days for a solid 6 weeks from just one planting. The tall, stiff green stems are topped with glittering silvery seed heads resembling fiber optic wands. For a summer-long harvest, plant three successions about a month apart. **How to grow:** Start seed indoors in trays 6 weeks before the last spring frost, and transplant outside after all danger of frost has passed. Space plants 12 inches (30 cm) apart. **Vase life tricks:** You can harvest seed heads at almost any stage, from barely emerging to fully open. The more mature the stem, the larger the explosion of seed heads. Stems last for 10 to 14 days in the vase; no floral preservative is needed.

MILLET I love this family of ornamental grasses and grow a wide variety of them every season. My favorites are 'Highlander', 'Red Jewel', and *Setaria macrostachya*. All are productive and easy to grow, and are a great addition to mixed bouquets. **How to grow:** Because millets are so quick to germinate in warm soil, I sow them directly in the soil outdoors (versus starting them in trays) every few weeks, from the last spring frost through early summer, so I have plenty all summer and autumn. **Vase life tricks:** Harvest anytime after the heads have emerged from their sheath, but before their color fades and they drop little seeds. Millets last an incredibly long time in the vase, up to 2 weeks if you use preservative. Seed heads can also be dried and used in arrangements—hang them upside down in a warm, dark place for a few weeks or until they have fully dried.

PANICUM MILIACEUM 'VIOLACEUM' This unique grass is one of my all-time favorites to grow and cut. The deep-green-and-black-tipped seed heads arch over from strong stems, resembling miniature, drooping broom corn. Their elegantly draped, tasseled blooms look amazing in late summer and autumn bouquets, producing abundantly for many weeks from one planting. **How to grow:** Start seed indoors in trays 6 weeks before the last spring frost, and transplant out after all danger of frost has passed. Space plants 12 inches (30 cm) apart. **Vase life tricks:** Seed heads can be harvested at almost any stage, from barely emerging to fully elongated. As stems ripen, they become longer and more deeply colored. Stems last for 7 to 10 days in the vase; no preservative is needed.

PENNISETUM VILLOSUM 'FEATHER TOP'

This beautiful grass has been a mainstay in my cutting garden for many years. One planting will flower for nearly 3 months, and the more you cut, the more it produces. The creamy white, fluffy seed heads look like they are dancing in the vase and are beautiful when combined with chrysanthemums and dahlias. **How to grow:** Start seed indoors in trays 6 weeks before the last spring frost, and transplant out after all danger of frost has passed. Space plants 12 inches (30 cm) apart. **Vase life tricks:** Seed heads should be harvested as soon as they've emerged. They will last for 7 to 10 days in the vase; no floral preservative is needed.

FIBER OPTIC GRASS

PENNISETUM VILLOSUM
'FEATHER TOP'

MILLET

PANICUM MILIACEUM
'VIOLACEUM'

PERENNIALS

Having a good supply of autumn-flowering perennials tucked into the garden allows you to make beautiful bouquets right up until the end of the growing season. Perennials' abundant flowering and low-maintenance personalities make them essentials for autumn. The varieties listed here are some of the easiest you can possibly grow and will reward you with buckets and buckets of flowers when the rest of the garden is starting to wane.

HOW TO GROW

Perennials are best planted in early autumn, at least 4 weeks before the first frost so they can get established before cold weather sets in. They can also be spring planted, but will be much less productive the first year than if they had gone in the previous autumn. Generally, perennials take 2 to 3 years to fully mature. Because they'll be in your garden for years, it's important to select a good site and keep weeds under control early on. After planting in the autumn, I apply a thick layer of mulch to the beds, at least 2 inches (5 cm) deep, to help keep weed seeds from germinating; then I monitor closely and stay on top of them in the spring. All of the plants listed here get quite big and require 12 to 18 inches (30 to 46 cm) of spacing to perform their best. Perennials are much harder to start from seed than annual plants, so start from already established plants. The varieties listed here grow quickly and are easy to divide and multiply. Unless specified, all do best in full sun.

FAVORITE VARIETIES

ASTERS For most of the year, these old-fashioned bloomers look like nothing more than a ferny clump of foliage. But once the days grow shorter and temperatures drop, perennial asters explode into an airy mass of star-shaped blooms that are a sight to behold. Their wispy stems make the perfect autumn bouquet filler, and they come in a wide range of colors, including blue, purple, white, rose, and magenta. I especially love 'Lady in Black', which has miniature blooms with cranberry centers and barely pink petals against gorgeous dark foliage. **Vase life tricks:** Pick when one-quarter of the flowers on a stem have opened, and place in water with floral preservative. You can expect a vase life of 5 to 7 days.

CHINESE LANTERN One of the most sought-after fall varieties I've ever grown, this unusual plant produces pod-covered stems that turn bright orange when the weather turns cold. These eye-catching cut flowers resemble traditional glowing lanterns from China and last for many years when dried. These plants are vigorous and spread by underground rhizomes, so unless you have an area where they can be free to wander, grow them in large pots. **Vase life tricks:** Harvest when the pods have changed to orange, cutting the stems off at ground level and removing all of the leaves. The stems will last for 2 to 3 weeks in a vase. To dry, hang upside down in a warm, dark place for a few weeks; once dried, they can last for years.

226

CHINESE LANTERN

ASTER

JAPANESE ANEMONE

SEDUM

JAPANESE ANEMONE Commonly referred to as windflowers for their elegant flowers that flutter in the breeze atop thin stems, these fall treasures bloom continuously for 2 or more months and come in a range of pastel colors, including white, rose, and purple. The flower shape of the varieties ranges from single to semi-double to double. Once established, anemones spread slowly by underground rhizomes and do best in light to medium shade, although plants can handle full sun if they get adequate water. There are dozens of varieties to choose from; I particularly love 'Honorine Jobert', with its sparkling white flowers and fluffy yellow stamens, and 'Robustissima'—its soft pink, single, cup-shaped flowers are more delicate than other autumn bloomers. **Vase life tricks:** Unlike most flowers, which should be picked when they are just opening, anemones must be harvested when fully open but before their pollen has started to shed; otherwise, they have a tendency to droop. As old blooms fade, others on the stem gradually open, and this long-lasting floral display will continue for a week in the vase if you use floral preservative.

SEDUM Also called stonecrop, this drought-tolerant, easy-to-grow landscape bloomer happens to make an amazing filler in late summer and early autumn bouquets. 'Autumn Joy' is the most commonly grown variety, but there are many other treasures worth seeking out, such as the brilliant hot pink 'Munstead Dark Red' and deep rose-red 'Autumn Fire'. **Vase life tricks:** You can cut and use sedums while their flowers are still green, when in full bloom, or even after they are done flowering, as the spent blooms work well in wreaths. As an added bonus, sedums have sturdy stems and a fantastic vase life of up to 2 weeks without preservative, and they are so wilt-proof you can use them out of water for a few days with good success.

230

PUMPKINS, SQUASH & GOURDS

My obsession with winter squash began many years ago when I worked at a produce stand during high school. Each autumn, as the weather turned cold and the leaves started to change, flatbed trucks filled with bins containing thousands of pumpkins, squash, and gourds in every shape, size, and color imaginable would roll into the parking lot. I was charged with decorating the stand and helping to set up the huge displays out front.

When my husband and I bought our house, one of the first things I planted in the garden was a bunch of winter squash, and every year I add new favorites to my already overflowing list. In addition to making beautiful ornaments, many make for fine eating. If you can make the room, they are definitely worth cultivating.

HOW TO GROW

Squash are heavy feeders, requiring soil rich in organic matter to thrive and produce abundantly. When preparing the ground, I add a few extra shovelfuls of compost to each planting hole, along with an extra scoop of balanced fertilizer, and mix them into the soil well.

Unlike other cutting garden additions that are grown tightly together in closely spaced rows, squash do best planted some distance apart in hills. One of the biggest mistakes many beginning growers make is not giving these rambling vines enough room to spread out. I space rows 6 feet (2 m) apart and give each plant 3 feet (1 m) on each side so that they can wander without getting crowded.

To get a head start, sow seed indoors 3 weeks before your last spring frost date. Plant 2 seeds per 4-inch (10-cm) pot, and transplant outside after all danger of frost has passed. Starting seeds indoors helps protect young seedlings from hungry rodents, birds, and cold, wet weather, which can cause them to rot. But seeds can be direct sown into the garden too, 2 seeds per hole, planted 1 inch (2.5 cm) deep, after all danger of frost has passed.

It's important to keep an eye on young plants and monitor them for slug damage during the spring months. I apply Sluggo, an organic slug repellent, at planting time and then after every hard rain. This repellent keeps the plants safe from the slimy predators but is safe for animals and children.

Once summer has arrived and plants start to take off, they require very little care. You can basically stand back and watch them grow.

FAVORITE VARIETIES

'CHIRIMEN' This darling little gem starts out dark emerald green, with subtle yellow flecks, but over time morphs into a warm buff color that's absolutely stunning. It's a great squash for eating, too.

'GALEUX D'EYSINES' One of the most unusual-looking varieties I've ever grown, this warm peach-colored squash is covered in a thick layer of rough-textured light brown warts. People either love it or are slightly repulsed by it. I belong to the first camp.

233

$1 lb

'CHIRIMEN'

'GALEUX D'EYSINES'

'MARINA DI CHIOGGIA' The deep blue-green rind of this eye-catching variety is covered in a thick layer of bubbly, warty bumps that make it look more like a geode than a squash. A must-grow for both eating and display.

'MUSQUE DE PROVENCE' Over time, the dark green rind of this medium-sized, deeply lobed pumpkin transforms into the most incredible warm chocolate brown. Wonderful for eating and as a long-lasting decoration.

'ROUGE VIF D'ETAMPES' Few pumpkins can rival the beauty of this flaming orange-red French variety. Also known as the Cinderella pumpkin, these gems resemble the pumpkin that Cinderella's fairy godmother transformed into her carriage.

'TRIAMBLE' My favorite squash variety, this stunning shamrock-shaped treasure is an exquisite shade of glowing blue-green. Not only are the fruit beautifully colored, nicely sized, and uniquely shaped, but after harvest they also generally last a year or more on display. I've even had a few make it past 2 years!

HARVEST TRICKS

For the longest shelf life and best coloring, it's important to harvest squash at the proper stage, before the first frost arrives. Once the stems begin to brown and the rind takes on dullness, check the fruits' maturity by pressing your fingernail into the rind—if it doesn't puncture, it's ready to pick. Remove the fruit from the plant with a sharp knife or pruners, leaving a piece of the vine attached at the top. Support the fruit from below and take special care to not break off the stem.

Clean freshly harvested fruit with a 10-percent bleach-to-water solution and place them out on tables in the garage or greenhouse to dry. Cure them for 2 to 3 weeks in a warm, dry place, then use the fruit for creating beautiful displays. If properly cured, most squash will last at least 3 months, but don't be surprised if they persist even longer.

'MARINA DI CHIOGGIA'

'MUSQUE DE PROVENCE'

'ROUGE VIF D'ETAMPES'

'TRIAMBLE'

SUNFLOWERS

It's no wonder that sunflowers have long held the top spot as the most widely grown cut flower worldwide—they are ridiculously easy to grow, thrive during the dog days of summer and early autumn, bloom abundantly, and require very little attention to thrive.

When my children were small, I would give them each a packet of mixed sunflower seeds in the spring and have them plant them around the perimeter of our family's vegetable garden. I vividly remember their chubby little fingers pressing the big striped seeds into the freshly prepared soil, so carefully and with such focus. After a few days of sunny weather, the seedlings would burst through the soil, and they'd be over the moon with excitement. No other flower brings such joy.

HOW TO GROW

One of the easiest flowers to grow, sunflowers can be either direct seeded or transplanted into the garden as soon as the weather has warmed and all threat of frost has passed. Seeds germinate rapidly, and within a few days plants will be poking out of the ground. If birds and other wildlife are an issue, be sure and protect young seedlings until they are 3 to 4 inches (7 to 10 cm) tall, since critters will make short work of pulling out young plants and eating the tender seeds if given the chance. I cover freshly seeded beds with frost cloth and anchor the corners down with heavy stones to keep the birds away until the plants have had a chance to root in and anchor themselves. To avoid this extra step, you can plant out transplants instead of seeds.

There are two types of sunflowers, branching and nonbranching. Branching types get quite large and produce an abundance of blooms over a long period of time. They require a good deal of room, so space them

18 to 24 inches (45 to 60 cm) apart. To stagger the harvest, sow a new batch every 3 to 4 weeks from spring through midsummer.

Nonbranching types (also called single stem) produce one flower per seed and are prized for their fast bloom time and long, straight stems. These are the types that most flower farmers choose to cultivate. To keep them at a manageable size, it's best to plant them quite close together; otherwise, you'll end up with broomstick-sized stems that are impossible to work into arrangements. For smaller, bouquet-sized blooms, space plants 4 to 6 inches (10 to 15 cm) apart. For a continuous harvest, sow successive plantings of these every 7 to 10 days throughout the spring and early summer.

FAVORITE VARIETIES

When choosing varieties for cut flowers, it's important to look for pollenless types. It's a shame to ruin a perfectly good tablecloth with a cloud of messy yellow pollen.

NONBRANCHING VARIETIES

'PROCUT BICOLOR' No other sunflower says fall quite like this beauty. The bloom's warm brown center is surrounded by a striking ring of bicolor gold and rusty red petals that look amazing mixed with grasses, amaranth, and other sunflowers.

'SUNRICH GOLD' One of our most abundantly grown varieties, this winner flowers just 60 to 70 days from sowing. While the entire Sunrich Series is worth cultivating, I particularly love Gold, with its clear yellow petals and pretty greenish yellow center.

238

'GREENBURST'

'PROCUT BICOLOR'

'CHOCOLATE'

'STARBURST PANACHE'

'SUNRICH GOLD'

'SUNRICH ORANGE'

'SUNRICH ORANGE' This garden treasure is fast to flower and is exactly what you expect in a sunflower: school bus–yellow petals and a thick, brown center. I love to combine this flower with dark foliage like ninebark and Chim Chiminee rudbeckia.

BRANCHING VARIETIES

'CHOCOLATE' This tall, highly branching variety is always a favorite with florists. The flower's dark chocolate petals and black centers add depth and intrigue to bouquets. I love mixing these sunflowers with other dark ingredients for a conversation-starting arrangement. Unlike most sunflowers, the darker petaled varieties have a tendency to drop their petals if cut when totally open, so be sure to harvest this beauty as soon as the petals start to unfurl.

'GREENBURST' I adore this cheerful double, early blooming variety with its fluffy yellow petals around a clear, bright green center. Flowering just 2 months from seeding, this cutie can be succession sown from early spring through mid-summer for flowers from early summer through late autumn.

'STARBURST PANACHE' I've grown dozens of sunflowers over the years, and none has ever outdone this one. Its ultrafluffy, shaggy petals and dark green-brown centers make for the most fantastic display. They are the epitome of autumn and look incredible displayed en masse.

VASE LIFE TRICKS

Harvest as soon as the first petals on a sunflower bloom start to unfurl, and strip the bottom three-fourths of the leaves from the stem for the longest vase life. No flower preservative is needed.

VINES

One of my favorite tricks for taking a simple arrangement to the next level is adding a few stems of a vine to the mix. There's something about these rambling, wild growers that brings a hint of whimsy to any type of arrangement.

Over the years I've experimented with a number of climbers, and while all are lovely, there are a handful—including both perennial and annual types—that have become permanent residents in my garden.

HOW TO GROW PERENNIAL VINES

Plant perennial vines in the autumn or early spring, and give these climbers room to roam and a sturdy trellis, arbor, or other structure to attach themselves to. These varieties are vigorous and don't require any special treatment other than being cut back to the ground every autumn.

FAVORITE PERENNIAL VARIETIES

CLEMATIS Once you've discovered this incredible group of plants, you'll want to own every single variety. I've grown more than 40 cultivars over the years, but there are two rampant growers that I find the most reliable for a steady supply of cutting material. 'Sweet Autumn' produces the most beautiful small, pure white, fragrant flowers during the later part of the summer and into autumn. As the flowers fade, they are followed by a silvery mass of airy seed heads. 'Bill MacKenzie' is another winner, with finely cut leaves that are smothered in a sea of golden lantern-shaped flowers for most of the summer. But the best part of the display comes in the autumn, when its silvery seedpods begin to emerge and sparkle like glitter in the late afternoon sun. **Vase life tricks:** Cut clematis will easily last for a week in water if you use preservative.

HOPS One of the first vines I ever planted, this foolproof climber is always a great conversation starter and will hide an unsightly building or telephone pole in a few short years. Hops vines come in both green and gold and produce a spectacular display of pendulous, chartreuse, cone-shaped flowers from late summer through early autumn. They make an excellent addition to large arrangements and also look amazing strung over a doorway or an arch, or hung from the ceiling above a dining table. **Vase life tricks:** Stems will last for about 5 days in water with preservative and can be displayed dry for up to 24 hours before starting to look tired.

HOW TO GROW ANNUAL VINES

Start seed indoors in pots 6 to 8 weeks before the last spring frost and transplant out after all danger of frost has passed. These annual climbers are very sensitive to cold, so wait until the weather has warmed before transplanting into the garden. Provide a strong trellis or support for vines to climb.

FAVORITE ANNUAL VARIETIES

CUP-AND-SAUCER VINE (*Cobaea scandens*) This vigorous climber is a beautiful addition to the garden and the vase. From late summer through the first autumn frost, vines are smothered in creamy white or deep purple cup-shaped flowers that seem to glow from within. Individual blossoms can be floated in shallow bowls, or vines can be incorporated into shorter arrangements. **Vase life tricks:** Pick flowers as they are just opening and sear the stem ends in boiling water for 7 to 10 seconds. Expect 4 to 5 days of vase life if floral preservative is used.

CUP-AND-SAUCER VINE

CLEMATIS

LOVE IN A PUFF VINE

NASTURTIUM 'GLEAM SALMON'

HOPS

LOVE IN A PUFF VINE (*Cardiospermum halicacabum*) Few vines rival the delicate beauty of this one in full bloom. The long, ferny-leaved vines are loaded with tiny white blossoms, and the intriguing green, balloonlike pods resemble miniature paper lanterns. What is even more magical is that inside each balloon are tiny black seeds imprinted with perfect white hearts. These vigorous growers will scramble up and over a trellis in a couple of months. **Vase life tricks:** Choose stems that have firmed up and are covered in little green lanterns. Cut foliage is prone to wilting in the heat, so harvest during the coolest part of the day and place directly into water to rest for a few hours before arranging. Stems will last for a week in the vase if you use flower preservative.

NASTURTIUM 'GLEAM SALMON' After years of hunting for a great trailing nasturtium in peach and pastel colors, I finally discovered the elusive 'Gleam Salmon'. This rambler is loaded with a profusion of creamy, salmon-peach blossoms all summer long. The flowers add interest and movement to larger-scale arrangements. **Vase life tricks:** Harvest flowers just as they are opening. If using the foliage, pick individual leaves or full vines once they become leathery or firm to the touch. Both flowers and foliage will persist for 7 to 10 days in the vase, even longer if you use preservative.

Autumn Projects

AUTUMNAL WREATH

One of the best ways to embrace the fading days of autumn is by capturing the fleeting magic in a large, showy display. Each autumn as we put the garden to bed, I set aside special bits and pieces of fruiting branches and pods and turn them into wild seasonal wreaths. Unlike their evergreen counterparts, which are meant to be full and lush, these twiggy creations are intended to represent the unruly nature of the season.

YOU WILL NEED

Pruners

Twenty to twenty-five 8-inch (20-cm) pieces of floral or paddle wire

Three 6- to 8-foot (1.8- to 2.4-m) pieces of fresh grapevine, leaves removed

Three 3- to 4-foot (0.9- to 1.2-m) lengths of bittersweet, leaves removed

10 to 15 branches of large-fruited rose hips, such as those from *Rosa dupontii*

15 to 20 stems of small-fruited rose hips, such as those from 'Sally Holmes' and *Rosa glauca*

18 to 20 stems of Chinese lanterns

1 To create the base for your wreath, form the grapevine into a circle. Secure the shape by wrapping a piece of wire around the vine where the ends meet. Add the next length of vine, wrapping it around the first. Finish by wrapping the final piece of vine around the others and secure them all together with wire. This will give you a sturdy base to build the wreath on.

2 One by one, wrap the bittersweet lengths evenly around the grapevine base, tucking the ends into the base to secure them.

3 Wire the larger stems of rose hips to the vine base, spacing each cluster evenly.

4 Tuck the small-fruited rose hips throughout the wreath by poking them into the little gaps in the vine base, especially on the outside perimeter so that they can be more easily seen.

5 Add the Chinese lanterns by poking them into the viney base. Place them evenly throughout the wreath for the most abundant look.

DUTCH STILL LIFE

Every autumn, as the chrysanthemum patch explodes into its typical overwhelming display, a new surge of creativity strikes, and it's impossible for me to stay focused on any task at hand. Few flowers can rival the lush, textural beauty of this amazing plant family's blossoms, and the fact that they come into bloom as the rest of the garden is fading makes them even more special.

Inspired by moody Dutch still-life paintings, this bouquet is a modern take on the old classics. The combination of fall-toned foliage, fruiting branches, and richly colored chrysanthemums makes a dramatic, memorable display.

YOU WILL NEED

Flower frog

A large ceramic bowl 12 inches (30 cm) in diameter

Floral putty

6 to 8 branches of beech foliage

3 or 4 multileaved stems of grape foliage

6 to 8 branches of viburnum foliage

5 to 7 arching rose hip stems

7 to 10 small-flowered branching chrysanthemums, such as 'Bronze Fleece'

7 to 10 branching sprays of large-flowered chrysanthemums, such as 'Heather James'

5 to 7 sprays of spiderlike chrysanthemums, such as 'Seaton's Toffee'

5 sprays of miniature fruited rose hips

1 Anchor the flower frog to the base of the bowl by applying a ring of floral putty to the bottom of the frog and pressing it firmly into the vase. The frog will help anchor the heavy branches and mums that would other-wise topple out of the low container.

2 Fill the bowl three-quarters full with water mixed with floral preservative.

3 Establish the overall shape of the arrangement. Place arching beech branches at 3 points in the vase to create a scalene triangle (with unequal sides), with a taller cluster of branches in the back left, a medium arching cluster on the right, and a low cascading display in front center. Make sure they are all securely inserted into the frog so that they don't fall out.

4 Add the grape foliage, echoing the beech placement.

5 Place the viburnum branches, again mimicking the placement of the beech, but making sure that the stems are a bit shorter. This will help create a foliage "nest" for the flowers

6 Add the arching stems of rose hips, echoing the shape of the foliage already in place. Make sure the hips stick out beyond the other ingredients enough so that they are visible. Also place a stem or two around the lip of the bowl.

7 Tuck in the airy sprays of small chrysanthemums throughout the bouquet, filling in the gaps between foliage. Continue to echo the asymmetrical shape.

8 Place the large, showy chrysanthemums. The big focal blooms need room, so take your time when placing them and be sure to turn some of them in different directions for a more natural, free-form look. Let a few spill down over the lip of the bowl and also out over the sides for a truly abundant effect.

9 Add in some sprays of spiderlike chrysanthemums among the larger, fuller blooms. This will add a beautiful texture to the arrangement.

10 Tuck in a few stems of small-fruited rose hips for a final bit of sparkle.

VINCENT VAN GOGH

As summer fades and early autumn arrives, sunflowers are in their prime, and there's no better way to usher in the changing seasons than by creating a wild, textural arrangement filled with the best of what the garden has to offer.

For this bouquet, inspired by Vincent van Gogh's famous *Sunflowers* painting, no special technique is required. You just need an arm-load of seasonal bounty to arrange in a hand-thrown pottery vessel.

YOU WILL NEED

A large vase with a tapered neck (12 inches/30 cm tall)

Pruners or clippers

6 full stems of amaranth 'Hot Biscuits'

5 stems of 'ProCut Bicolor' or other bicolor sunflowers

6 stems of 'Chocolate' or other dark sunflowers

8 branching stems of rudbeckia such as Cherokee Sunset Mix

8 stems of rudbeckia such as Chim Chiminee Mix

15 stems of millet (*Setaria macrostachya*)

1 Fill the vase three-quarters full with water mixed with floral preservative. Place the brown amaranth stems in the vase, cutting some shorter and leaving some longer, encouraging them to cascade over the edges, so that they create a loose foliage frame for the other ingredients.

2 Add the bicolor sunflowers, nestling them in among the amaranth.

3 Weave in the dark sunflowers, filling in the spaces between the amaranth and other sunflowers.

4 Add the branching Cherokee Sunset rudbeckia evenly throughout the arrangement, so that they arch out over the sides of the bouquet.

5 Thread in the Chim Chiminee rudbeckia, filling in any remaining holes in the bouquet. These spiky blooms add an airy element that breaks up the heaviness of the other, chunkier ingredients.

6 Place the millet throughout the bouquet, making sure that the small-flowered seed heads are high enough above the other stems to be seen.

257

WIN

TER

WINTER STILLNESS

Winter is always a welcome reprieve after the long and busy flower growing season. While snow is rare here in Washington, the gray skies, bone-chilling cold, and relentless rains drive even the most stalwart gardener inside. I'm forced to get much-needed downtime and recharge before the next season begins.

In early winter, I spend dry days outside foraging for evergreens and interesting bits for our annual holiday wreath-and-garland-making extravaganza. When it's rainy, my family and I are inside by the woodstove, creating festive swags, wreaths, and hundreds of feet of handmade garland. The scent of pine hangs heavy in the air, and our hands are permanently stained and sticky from mud and sap. We pull potted paperwhites and amaryllises out of the basement and dole these out over the winter months, both as gifts and to keep the house filled with fresh flowers and fragrance.

Once the craziness of the holidays passes, I'm truly able to settle down. Each day's walk to the mailbox brings a new batch of seed catalogs, and my imagination runs wild with all of the possibilities for the coming year. Graph paper, gardening books, catalogs, and colored pencils litter my dining room table, and every waking hour is devoted to plotting out the season to come.

261

Winter
Tasks

TAKE STOCK AND CLEAN

To me, nothing is better for the mind or soul than to clean and tidy your workspace before beginning a new project. On rare days when the sun peeks out from behind the clouds, I make a break for the propagation greenhouse and start the slow process of reconciling our supplies and noting what needs fixing or replacing for the season to come. I take stock of everything, from fertilizer to seed trays, plant tags, and soil. Then I give the space a deep cleaning, which includes washing out all of the seeds trays with bleach water, organizing all of the remaining supplies, and putting everything in its rightful place.

PLAN THE GARDEN

Before diving headfirst into garden planning, I spend some time going through my old boxes of seeds, cleaning out empty packets, checking quantities, and reorganizing everything that remains. Then I pull out last season's garden notebooks and review what worked, what didn't, and what changes I want to make in the season to come. In the "Basics" chapter of this book, I explain how to plan, plant, and organize your cutting garden for a season's worth of flowers. Be sure to reference it before creating your own garden plan.

ORDER SEEDS AND SUPPLIES

To ensure the best seed selection, I highly advise that you order early. Over the years, I've missed out on a lot of great plants because I ordered too late. But be sure to prioritize: with dozens of seed and supply catalogs arriving each week, it's easy to get swept up in the excitement of the coming season and order way too much. While I give myself pretty loose reins when choosing varieties, there does come a point where too much of a good thing becomes a problem. So, keep in mind your time and space limitations to help prevent overordering, overspending, and feeling overwhelmed.

PLANT BARE ROOTS

One of my favorite winter tasks is choosing and planting bare-root shrubs and trees. Compared to potted shrubs and trees, bare-root stock is generally larger (yet much lighter than a potted plant's weight), only a fraction of the price, and much less likely to experience transplant shock. Whenever possible, opt for buying bare-root plants, even though the window of availability is quite short (generally about 6 to 8 weeks). If you can't plant your bare-root choices in the ground immediately, they should be "heeled in," which means to temporarily bury the roots in either plain soil or a pile of moist wood chips until planting time to ensure the roots do not dry out. Soak bare-root stock for 24 hours before planting.

CARE FOR TOOLS

In the early days of my farming career, a very successful grower told me that investing in well-made tools and caring for them properly would serve me for many, many years to come. And he was right: having the right tools for the job makes all the difference. Not only can you get everything done faster and with more ease, but using the proper tools is also kinder to your body. Each winter I make it a point to give every tool in the arsenal a once-over. I clean, oil, and sharpen all blades, forks, and pruners. I also thoroughly clean all wooden handles and apply boiled linseed oil to maintain the wood's luster and prevent splintering and discoloration. Then I return everything to its spot in the shed.

PRUNE

Midwinter is the ideal time to prune deciduous woody shrubs and ornamental trees. With the plants bare, it's much easier to assess their condition and work efficiently. Begin by removing any dead, diseased, or damaged wood and then move on to taking out thin, weak stems. If you find suckers sprouting from the base of a plant, remove those as well. Then move on to pruning for visual appeal, keeping in mind the natural shape of the plant when making final cuts. I generally begin with the most time-consuming varieties, like roses and PeeGee hydrangeas, move on to cane berries and deciduous shrubs, and finish with fruiting trees.

EXTEND THE SEASON

I can't stress enough how much you'll benefit from growing cut flowers in greenhouses, or another form of cover, during the winter months. You'll have blooms with longer, stronger stems, which are better for arranging; higher bloom quality; lower risk of plant disease; and the ability to get a jump on the season. Covered flowers bloom, and are ready for cutting, up to 6 weeks earlier than uncovered field crops. While most gardeners don't have the space or budget for a large greenhouse, there are a number of affordable, creative options available.

High tunnels, or hoop houses, are essentially unheated greenhouses that are tall enough to walk in. They can be purchased as kits (see "Resources," page 304) or made from scratch with the help of a pipe bender and some strong friends. This type of structure is ideal for setting up a propagation space to start seeds, extend the shoulder seasons, and grow varieties like dinner plate dahlias and lisianthus that need a little extra protection or heat.

For home gardeners with limited space, or growers with a limited budget, low tunnels are an ideal choice because they can be erected in a very short amount of time, can be rotated over different planting beds throughout the season, are very easy for just one person to ventilate, take up a minimal amount of room, and are quite resistant to wind and snow.

267

START SEEDS

Few things are more exciting to me than ripping open the first packet of seeds at the start of a new growing season. While we plant the majority of seeds in early spring, I advise doing this in late winter if you live in a warmer climate or have heated propagation space. In late winter, I start seeds that are slow to germinate, like perennials and lisianthus, along with any sweet peas that weren't sown in autumn, and early blooming, cold-tolerant annuals like Iceland poppies and snapdragons, as well as larkspur, love-in-a-mist, and false Queen Anne's lace that weren't sown in autumn.

—

Winter Berries, Blooms & Foliage

—

AMARYLLISES

Few other flowers can contend with an amaryllis in full bloom: the magnificence and grandeur of this flowering gem is nearly impossible to ignore and even more impossible to forget. While amaryllises are actually tropical plants, native to South America, you can force them into bloom indoors during the cold days of winter, and they will brighten a dark room like nothing else. One of the easiest bulbs to force, they need only bright light, good soil, consistent water, and a warm room to thrive. They also make wonderful holiday gifts.

Amaryllises come in a range of brilliant colors, including white, pink, salmon, coral, scarlet, orange, red, and many exquisite multicolored and striped varieties. I love to plant them in masses, filling large bowls with as many bulbs as I can fit. A mantel decorated with a line of potted amaryllises in full flower is nothing short of spectacular. I'm completely in love with this incredible plant, and once you get to know it, you will be, too.

HOW TO GROW

Amaryllis bulbs are quite expensive, but if you can swing it, buy the biggest ones available; I prefer the ³²/₃₄ cm size (the bulbs are sized by circumference). Smaller bulbs still put on a lovely show, and larger ones will produce 2 or 3 stems with 4 to 6 large flowers each. When selecting bulbs, look for those that are firm when squeezed and free of bruises or damage. If you don't intend to pot up your bulbs right away in autumn, store them in some type of breathable bag, in a cool, dark spot with temperatures ranging from 50° to 60°F (10° to 15.5°C).

To plant, select a pot with drainage holes that's at least twice the diameter and depth of the bulb. Fill your pot partway with good-quality potting soil, leaving 4 to 5 inches (10 to 13 cm) of room at the top, then nestle your bulb into place. Fill the rest of the pot with soil,

leaving just the neck of the bulb sticking out, then tamp down the soil firmly to secure the bulb. Water deeply and move the pot to a warm room, ideally with a temperature of 68° to 70°F (20°C). Check the soil every few days to make sure it stays moist but not soggy—water sparingly; otherwise, the bulbs will rot rather than root. Once a stem and leaves appear, water regularly, 2 or 3 times a week.

Depending on variety and the temperature in your space, amaryllises will generally bloom 5 to 8 weeks after planting, and will reach 18 to 24 inches (46 to 61 cm) tall. Bulbs planted in early winter will take a little longer to flower than those planted closer to spring.

Once the blooms open, move the pot out of direct sunlight to prolong flowering time and protect petals from fading. Fully open amaryllises can topple under their own weight, so be sure to stake the stems—I've returned to a pile of soil and shattered terra-cotta more than once because a large flower stalk leaned out a bit too far.

To extend the show, I stagger my plantings about 10 days apart, so as one batch is fading, the next is coming into bloom.

Amaryllises require a period of dormancy to bloom again, and with proper care they can be saved to flower in another year. After the blooms fade, move the plant to a sunny window and continue to water regularly. Once the danger of frost has passed, move it outdoors. Fertilize the plant monthly with a water-soluble fertilizer suited for potted plants, according to the directions on the package. Stop watering 12 to 14 weeks before you want it to bloom again. Bring inside and store dry at 50°F (10°C) for 8 weeks (this is the required length of dormancy). After that, repot the bulb based on the previous directions, and you will be blessed with flowers in just a few weeks.

269

FAVORITE VARIETIES

There are dozens and dozens of incredible amaryllis varieties to choose from. I'm on a personal quest to grow every single cultivar, but really, almost any one will do. The following are a few of my favorite discoveries so far.

'APPLEBLOSSOM' Massive pink-and-white flowers adorn this variety—they're reminiscent of crabapple blossoms in the spring, which start out as fat pink buds and open to snowy white petals. It's one of my absolute favorites.

'NYMPH' The fully double blossoms of this fairylike wonder are almost otherworldly. A combination of creamy white, painted with irregular veins of coral red, the bloom is so ruffled it could almost pass as a peony or garden rose on steroids.

'PEACH MELBA' The rich coral-peach, flared blooms are accented with deep orange veining on the petals radiating out from a rich orange center. It's a true showstopper.

'RED LION' This extremely vigorous variety is one of the most popular choices for Christmas. Its fire engine–red flowers are often borne in clusters of 4 or 5 buds and look striking against a dark backdrop of evergreens.

'SWEET NYMPH' Fully double, deep rose-pink flowers are accented with darker veins and light pink edges, making for a truly exquisite show.

VASE LIFE TRICKS

Amaryllises make excellent, long-lasting cut flowers that can last for nearly 3 weeks in a vase. Be sure to add them to an arrangement while they're still in bud, though, because fully opened blossoms will bruise easily and show signs of damage as they unfurl. Stems will often collapse under their own weight while still in bloom. To prevent this, slip a long, thin bamboo skewer down through the large hollow stem and secure it in place with a cotton ball.

'RED LION'

'PEACH MELBA'

'NYMPH'

'APPLEBLOSSOM'

'SWEET NYMPH'

BERRIES
& BLOOMS

For much of the year, I can literally step off my back porch and harvest an armload of flowers, foliage, or berries within seconds. But despite my best efforts to stock the garden and greenhouses with nearly year-round growers, I, too, struggle to get enough interesting material in winter.

As the garden goes to sleep, I kick myself if I don't have plants that produce during this season. So, in autumn, I make it a point to put in some extragenerous rows of my favorite greens, berries, and blooming shrubs, including both pink and white andromeda, blue-berried privet, and some viburnum 'Spring Bouquet'. While it takes a few years after planting for you to be able to harvest any real abundance from them, the wait is worth it. Remember, you can always buy cut greenery while yours is growing in.

The varieties that follow are the ones that I'm most often knocking on doors asking to cut or foraging from abandoned lots around town. During the height of summer, I might pass over these greens for something more showy or bold, but during the frigid months, they are just the ticket for adding interest to my creations and really are worth their weight in gold.

Along with those listed, English holly is a must-have for me in winter. It can be slow or hard to grow, and can be invasive in some areas, so it's best to just buy cut holly greens from your local garden center or wholesaler during the holiday season. I particularly love holly with either yellow or white variegated foliage; they make an interesting accent to wreaths and garlands. The solid green-leaved type with scarlet berries is always a popular choice for holiday decorations, too. Be sure to wear thick gloves when handling holly, though, because their leaves are superthorny.

FAVORITE VARIETIES

ANDROMEDA (*Pieris japonica*) If you've ever encountered a fully blooming bush, then you know just how spectacular this plant is. Long cascading flower panicles in either ivory or rose cover exquisite evergreen foliage from winter through early spring. Flowers cut while in bud, before they've fully opened, will last longer than those cut in full bloom. **How to grow:** Andromedas prefer cool summers and dappled shade, and need to be planted in acidic soil. While slow growing, they are beautiful in the landscape and thrive in shadier corners of the garden where many plants do not. Plant during the autumn in mild climates, in spring elsewhere, and mulch around the base of young shrubs with 2 to 4 inches (5 to 10 cm) of compost or wood chips.

CAMELLIA (*Camellia japonica* and *Camellia sasanqua*) These are old garden favorites in the southern United States, and nothing quite compares to a mature one in full bloom. While the roselike blossoms don't hold particularly well once cut, they can last for up to 5 days if harvested early, either in swollen bud or shortly after the flowers emerge, and kept out of direct sunlight. I find that they make an excellent addition to winter arrangements that don't have to last too long, such as those for an event or holiday celebration. **How to grow:** This shade-loving shrub thrives in acidic soil and can be planted anytime during the autumn in mild

climates or spring elsewhere. Avoid areas with cold, drying winds, as this will desiccate the foliage in the winter. For new shrubs, add 3 to 4 inches (7.6 to 10 cm) of compost or wood chips as insulating mulch around the base of the plant.

IVY Where I live, English ivy grows extremely well—so well, in fact, that it has actually become a noxious weed. In winter, I harvest buckets of it from abandoned lots all over town. The greenish yellow flowers look amazing in wreaths and centerpieces, and as spring approaches, the flowers transform into beautiful deep blue berries that look smashing in garlands and bouquets. There are many varieties with interesting leaves, including both white and gold variegation, that are much less invasive. I love twining these bicolored leaves through wreaths for added interest and, during wedding season, using their sturdy vines as a base for flower girl crowns. Harvest anytime after the flowers have dropped their pollen and started to form green pods and/ or blue berries. **How to grow:** This wandering vine should be planted with caution (check with your state's noxious weed control organization for guidance in your location). I grow it in a collection of large pots on my back patio so that it doesn't spread by runners in my own garden. Plant in the spring and grow in full sun.

PRIVET (*Ligustrum japonicum*) This is hands down my favorite winter berry of all time. It has beautiful sprays of sturdy, blue-black berries that persist through even the most brutal winter weather. I planted a 100-foot (30.5-m) long row of privet because there just never seems to be enough to last the entire winter. The berries are as tough as nails and can hold out of water without shriveling for many weeks. **How to grow:** Privet is easy to grow and tolerates a wide range of soils, making it a must-grow if you can find a place to tuck in a few shrubs. Plant anytime during the autumn in mild climates or spring elsewhere, and for new shrubs, add 3 to 4 inches (7.6 to 10 cm) of compost or wood chips around the base of the plant.

VIBURNUM 'SPRING BOUQUET' This versatile winter-flowering beauty is loaded with pinkish red buds and soft white blossoms that turn to shiny blue berries from midwinter through early spring. The foliage, fruit, and blooms are especially great in Valentine's Day arrangements. **How to grow:** Able to grow in most soils, in both sun and shade, this sweet shrub is a wonderful addition to the cutting garden. Plant anytime during autumn in mild climates or spring elsewhere; for new shrubs, add 3 to 4 inches (7.6 to 10 cm) of compost or wood chips around the base of the plant.

WINTERBERRY (*Ilex verticillata*) These typically produce showy red berries, but with a little searching, you can find both orange- and golden-berried varieties, too. While fruiting stems can take a few light freezes, harvest them in early winter to prevent the berries from being damaged by extreme cold. **How to grow:** Winterberry thrives in wet, acidic soils with lots of organic matter, in full sun to partial shade. Plant in autumn in mild climates or spring elsewhere. They require a pollinator to set fruit—a good rule of thumb is to plant 1 male for every 20 females. Consult your local garden center for their recommended varieties and pollinators best suited for your area.

VASE LIFE TRICKS

When cut for their foliage and flowers, all of these varieties will last a week and often much longer in the vase, especially if you add flower preservative to the water. If harvesting for the berries, you can expect them to last for 2 weeks in or out of water.

ANDROMEDA

WINTERBERRY

IVY

CAMELLIA

VIBURNUM 'SPRING BOUQUET'

PRIVET

BRANCHES FOR WINTER FORCING

While the garden is still fast asleep, I like to bring a burst of energy indoors. So, in midwinter, I stroll through the garden and collect a few buckets of branches for forcing, which means getting them to bloom ahead of their natural cycle. While most woody, deciduous trees or shrubs that bloom in early spring are good candidates for forcing, I've had the greatest success with the old-fashioned go-to's that follow because they are fast to flower, last in the vase, and grow abundantly in most climates.

When choosing stems for cutting, look for ones with buds that are swollen and, if possible, showing some color. Using sharp, heavy-duty pruners, harvest stems and immediately place in a bucket of warm water with flower preservative mixed in. When transferring to your final vase, be sure to recut the stems so that they will continue to drink, and add preservative to the water. You want to recreate a spring environment and trick the branches into flowering, so the warmer and brighter your space, the faster the flowers will open. Just keep them out of direct sun. If they're taking too long to open, you can place a plastic garbage bag over the tops of the branches, and mist a few times a day to create humidity until the buds begin to color and swell.

FAVORITE VARIETIES

APRICOT, CHERRY, PEACH, AND PLUM

(*Prunus*) So many varieties, both fruiting and ornamental, in the *Prunus* genus make excellent candidates for forcing. If you don't have a large enough property to plant these medium-sized trees, connecting with a local orchard during peak pruning season is an excellent way to acquire some extra branches. Flowering plums, with either pink or white blooms, are among my favorites for cutting. Both peaches and apricots have pink flowers, and if forced early enough, are gorgeous in Valentine's Day bouquets. (While cherries are in the *Prunus* genus, they're not well suited to forcing, since their blooms need more time to mature—though I love using them in spring, so I have included them there.) **How to grow:** These trees prefer full sun and well-drained, slightly acidic soil. Flower blossoms will develop on branches' previous year's growth, so don't prune too heavily, so as not to impact next year's blossom display. **How to force bloom:** Most *Prunus* varieties can be harvested in very tight bud with little to no color showing, or when buds are swollen and have started to color. Either way, cut and immediately place in water with flower preservative, then move to a cool, bright room. Stems harvested in midwinter can take 2 to 3 weeks to open, whereas stems picked in late winter will take only 7 to 10 days. Stems will last in the vase for more than 2 weeks.

FLOWERING QUINCE (*Chaenomeles*) I have a bit of a love/hate relationship with flowering quince. Its thorny stems are tricky to harvest without getting pricked, but it's also one of the earliest and showiest blooms that can be forced inside, and you can pick stems over a very long period, from midwinter through early spring. I prefer *Chaenomeles speciosa* varieties because their upright growth and large floriferous stems work very well in bouquets. 'Snow' has large, snow-white

APRICOT, CHERRY, PEACH, AND PLUM

FLOWERING QUINCE

FORSYTHIA

WILLOW

blooms, 'Geisha Girl' has pale apricot petals, and my all-time favorite, 'Rubra', boasts bright scarlet/coral flowers that light even the darkest day. **How to grow:** Flowering quince is hardy and can tolerate a wide range of soil types; it takes up to 5 years to reach maturity. Grow in full sun. If you need to prune, do it in the summer; this promotes spur formation, which leads to a more generous floral display down the road. **How to force bloom:** Harvest stems when buds are swollen and colored, then place in water with flower preservative and bring them into a cool, bright room to open. If they are cut with immature buds, the flower blossoms will be paler than those cut when they're more mature. Depending on the stage of harvest, stems can last for up to 2 weeks.

FORSYTHIA One of the most commonly grown flowering shrubs—and quite possibly the easiest to force—is forsythia, whose vibrant school bus–yellow blossoms explode in the dead of winter when little else is available. While I have a small row of forsythia tucked along the north border of my yard, I often scavenge extra branches from long-forgotten places like abandoned lots, where they won't be missed. **How to grow:** These plants couldn't be easier to grow; they seem to actually thrive on neglect, surviving for decades. They are drought resistant, can handle most temperature extremes, and also provide beautiful fall color in the landscape and vase. If you've inherited an old, nonproductive plant, shear it to the ground just after flowering and let new growth emerge. Established plants should be pruned regularly to maintain size and keep stems actively growing. Tuck new plants into the garden in autumn through early spring. **How to force bloom:** Harvest stems when buds start to swell in late winter, and place them in water with flower preservative in a cool room. Blossoms will emerge within 7 to 10 days.

WILLOW (*Salix*) For most of the year, the large stand of willows in my garden goes unnoticed. But every winter, after a spell of warm weather, the whole grove turns into a glistening fairyland as the fuzzy silver catkins are backlit by the late-day sun. I have a handful of varieties in the patch that I love, including the North American native *Salix discolor*, which can be found growing around many old homes; *Salix gracilistyla*, which produces long, pink-red-tinged catkins; and *Salix melanostachys*, with striking black catkins. **How to grow:** Willows are some of the easiest shrubs to cultivate. They thrive anywhere there is ample moisture and do well even in the poorest of soils. If left unchecked, they will quickly become small trees, so after the bushes have had a few years to establish, cut back the branches to the height you want the new growth to spring from. I generally cut them down to 3 to 4 feet (1 to 1.3 m) above the ground. Propagating willows couldn't be easier, and the winter months are the best time to do this. Stick 18- to 24-inch (46- to 60-cm) whips into the soil with 6 inches (15 cm) remaining above ground, and by late spring they will have rooted. **How to force bloom:** Because willows produce the showiest catkins on the second year's growth, I advise harvesting half of the branches each year so that you'll always have an abundant supply of stems for arranging. When catkins have swelled in late winter and the bud scales have dropped off, it's time to harvest. If picked at the proper stage, cut stems will last anywhere from 12 to 15 days. Willows also make an excellent dried flower. After the catkins have fully emerged from their scales, but before they begin to show yellow pollen, remove the stems from water and let them dry slowly in a cool room. Keep in mind that the catkins are fragile, so handle with care.

281

EVERGREEN CUTS

Here in Washington, nicknamed the Evergreen State, we are blessed with a lush, verdant landscape all winter long. The combination of generous rainfall and relatively mild temperatures creates the perfect environment for an abundant, diverse selection of evergreens. On our property, I harvest from our many large, well-established trees and shrubs, and I also supplement with both foraged and purchased greens.

Each winter as I gear up to make our seasonal projects, I call friends who have large patches of evergreen trees and shrubs and ask permission to cut from them in trade for a handmade wreath or garland of their choice. So far, I've never encountered a "no" using this tactic. Then, after a good early winter windstorm, my family and I cruise through a few local forests, picking up fallen branches on the side of the road. Next, I pay a visit to a big floral wholesaler and grab a few bales of varieties that don't grow in abundance on this side of the state, such as juniper and incense cedar. Finally, I raid my own garden and pick truckloads of scented greens, including two types of cedar, laurel, boxwood, bay, and holly.

Depending on what area you call home, there are surely a number of evergreen foliage plants from which you can cut. But before you head into the woods with loppers, go through the proper channels and acquire the necessary permits and/or permission from the landowners.

Planting a large tree—such as cedar, fir, pine, or spruce—with the idea that you'll use it for cutting will leave you disappointed. Trees take many years to mature enough for you to have a meaningful harvest

without disfiguring it. So, for purposes of including this kind of greenery in your arrangements, it makes the most sense to buy or forage for it.

Growing evergreen shrubs, though, is well worth the effort. In general, you should have enough greenery for cutting within 3 to 5 years.

FAVORITE VARIETIES

BOXWOOD Its foliage is unmatched in both sturdiness and beauty. I use it as a base for wreaths, swags, garlands, and arrangements. In the vase, it will last for up to 2 weeks, and out of water, it will stay looking great for over a month if displayed outside. **How to grow:** Boxwood prefers full sun to part shade and can handle a wide range of soil types. It is slow growing and generally takes 4 to 5 years to fully mature. Plant during the autumn in mild climates or spring elsewhere, and mulch around the base of young shrubs with 2 to 4 inches (5 to 10 cm) of compost or wood chips.

EUCALYPTUS The fragrant blue-gray foliage is a wonderful addition to bouquets, garlands, and wreaths. Cut stems will stay fresh for 3 to 4 weeks in the vase and then will dry perfectly in place. **How to grow:** Though technically a tree, it is grown as an annual by flower farmers all around the world, starting plants from seed in early spring so that they form 3-by-3-foot (91-by-91-cm) branchy shrubs by late autumn that can be harvested in early winter. If grown in the ground in a hoop house, or in pots in a minimally heated greenhouse, its foliage can be harvested well through the holiday season.

282

JAPANESE EUONYMUS

EUCALYPTUS

BOXWOOD

JUNIPER

JAPANESE EUONYMUS Its unique variegated leaves makes a wonderful accent to garlands and swags. Harvest foliage after it has become sturdy—generally after midsummer through autumn and winter. It will last for 2 weeks in the vase, and 1 week out of water. **How to grow:** This is easy to grow, vigorous, and thrives in most soil types; variegated forms grow more slowly than the green-leaved types. Plant during the autumn in mild climates or spring elsewhere, and mulch around the base of young shrubs with 2 to 4 inches (5 to 10 cm) of compost or wood chips.

JUNIPER Junipers are highly fragrant and sought after for their blue-green foliage and blue cones that resemble little blueberries. Their foliage turns a warm bronze in the winter, so be sure to pick before this happens for the best display. You can expect a 3- to 4-week vase life. **How to grow:** This scented treasure takes 4 to 5 years to establish, but makes a great addition to the garden if you have extra room. Plant during the autumn in mild climates or spring elsewhere, and mulch around the base of young shrubs with 2 to 4 inches (5 to 10 cm) of compost or wood chips.

VASE LIFE TRICKS

As far as cut flower material goes, all of these are exceptionally hardy. In a vase, change the water weekly for greatest longevity. To keep foliage looking its freshest indoors, you can mist it with water daily.

HELLEBORES

Hellebores have become all the rage with both floral designers and gardeners over the past few years. And it's no wonder: they are one of the few herbaceous perennials to bloom in the dead of winter. Available in a rainbow of muted colors, including eggplant, chartreuse, ivory, wine, crimson, peach, mauve, and even black—and with flowers in frilly doubles, speckled bicolors, delicately brush-marked picotees, and standard five-pointed stars—hellebores are both beautiful and incredibly diverse.

Poring over catalogs each year, I have the hardest time exercising restraint. Hellebores are expensive and take a few years to grow before they really start cranking out enough blooms to pick, so I highly recommend investing early on so you can build up a nice collection in your cutting garden. You'll be rewarded each successive winter with buckets of the prettiest blossoms.

HOW TO GROW

Hellebores are tough, easy to grow, and long lived, and require very little maintenance to thrive. Their thick, rough leaves also make them deer resistant. Most garden centers and nurseries readily stock these beauties, especially during the early spring months. While you might be tempted to purchase large pots so you'll have blooms to work with right away, I've found that choosing smaller, 4½-inch (11.5-cm) pots allows me to buy nearly twice as many for the same price. Smaller plants will take a few years longer to mature, however, so if you're in a hurry, then by all means go big.

Hellebores like shade and do well where other plants don't, such as under the outer rim of deciduous tree canopies, under larger deciduous shrubs, and on the north side of most buildings. Grow them in rich, organic soil, and don't let them sit in waterlogged ground for prolonged periods of time, as they can rot.

In early winter, right before flowers begin to emerge, sprinkle a fresh layer of compost around the base of the plants. This not only provides an extra dose of nutrients and mulch for weed suppression but also forms a dark, clean background that helps set off the blooms nicely. In late winter, when the plants begin to flower, remove older, blemished leaves to make sure the floral display is unmarred. This also makes way for new leaves that will emerge in the spring. Once you've got a collection of hellebores established, you'll never have a shortage of plants because they self seed readily each spring.

FAVORITE VARIETIES

There are many hellebores to choose from, and it can be tough to narrow down your wish list. Trust me, I know! But unless you are dying to become a plant collector, sticking with the easiest and fastest-flowering types will ensure the greatest success.

HELLEBORUS ARGUTIFOLIUS, the Corsican species, is hands down one of my favorite varieties to use in early spring bouquets. Its celery green, cup-shaped blooms open atop generous 3-foot (91-cm) stems, adding drama and stature to every arrangement.

HELLEBORUS FOETIDUS, the stinking hellebore, is also one of my favorites. While it does emit a slightly skunky fragrance, its long-stemmed, pale green flowers are edged with tiny bands of red and look amazing in arrangements.

287

HELLEBORUS FOETIDUS

HELLEBORUS ARGUTIFOLIUS

HELLEBORUS ORIENTALIS

HELLEBORUS ORIENTALIS, also known as Lenten rose, is the most commonly grown variety and comes in the widest range of bloom types, including stripes, doubles, and bicolors. They are the hardiest group, too, withstanding both cold and heat extremes. They self-sow freely and are great planted with other shade-loving, late winter flowers, such as snowdrops and wood anemones.

VASE LIFE TRICKS

Getting hellebores to last as cut flowers is simple, but requires you to have some self-control: you must select blooms at the proper stage; otherwise, they'll wilt within a few hours of picking. This means that while you may want to pick every flower as soon as it opens, you must wait until the blooms develop seedpods in the center. The more developed the seedpods, the sturdier the cut hellebore will be, and the longer it will last. A very mature hellebore bloom will hold up, nearly unscathed, out of water for an entire day, lending itself to wearable creations such a boutonnieres, corsages, and flower crowns. Flowers in the vase will last between 5 and 8 days.

PAPERWHITE NARCISSUSES

Paperwhite narcissuses, commonly known as paperwhites, are of one of the easiest and most rewarding bulbs you can grow. While mild-region gardeners can plant them outside in autumn, it's common in any climate to "force" them, meaning that you can prompt them to bloom indoors ahead of their usual early spring flowering time. During the cold, dark days of winter, their vibrant green foliage and large clusters of sweetly scented blooms will brighten any indoor space.

Because they are inexpensive, nearly foolproof to grow, and produce masses of fragrant flowers that I can enjoy when absolutely nothing else is alive in my garden, they have quickly become one of my favorite winter treats. Paperwhites are unique in that they don't require any cold temperatures to flower (as you'll learn in this book, many bulbs need a period of winter chilling to bloom). For impatient gardeners like me, these beauties are a must. I order large bags of paperwhite bulbs in the autumn and spend a solid day before the holidays filling every terra-cotta pot I can get my hands on with their fat golden bulbs. I then tuck the massive collection into a cool, frost-free spot in my garage, and pull out a few pots at a time over the course of the winter to keep our house filled with flowers. Potted paperwhites also make an excellent gift.

HOW TO GROW

Order bulbs in summer, and if you're like me and want flowers all winter long, buy them in bulk. Be sure to get the biggest, fattest bulbs you can find, because you'll be rewarded with 2 meaty stems per bulb. Store them in paper or mesh bags with plenty of air circulation, at room temperature, in a dark spot until planting in autumn. I prefer to pot them up all at once and then leave the majority of the pots in a cool, dark spot, such as a garage, basement, or outdoor shed that won't freeze, bringing a few at a time into the warm house so that I can stagger the flowering window throughout the winter months. It generally takes just 4 to 6 weeks from planting time until they're in full bloom.

Though you can grow paperwhites in glass bulb vases and bowls with stones or sand, I recommend growing them in soil. To do this, fill your pots halfway with soil, and set the bulbs in, spacing them tightly so they're nearly touching each other. Then fill the pots with soil so just the tips of the paperwhite necks are showing. Water well, and either set the pots out on display or tuck them away to enjoy later. I think paperwhites are most beautiful when displayed en masse. Once the plants reach 1 foot (30 cm) tall, they tend to become a bit leggy and floppy, so find something to stake them with as they grow. I love using craggy old apple branches and beautiful ribbons to prop and secure them upright.

If grown in a relatively cool room, 60° to 65°F (15.6° to 18°C), the flower display can last for up to a month, with each pot blooming for a few weeks. Be sure to water your paperwhites every few days, but avoid leaving them waterlogged, because the bulbs will rot.

FAVORITE VARIETIES

You'll find many paperwhite varieties; these are some of my top picks.

'CHINESE SACRED LILY' has creamy white petals with bright yellow centers and takes 6 to 8 weeks to flower.

'GALILEE' offers glowing white displays and flowers roughly 4 to 6 weeks after planting.

'GRAND SOLEIL D'OR' has bright yellow petals and takes 6 to 8 weeks to bloom.

'NIR' is a pure white beauty that is one of the earliest to flower.

'ZIVA' sports snowy white blooms; this is what I plant most often, because it's easy to find and blooms in 6 weeks.

'CHINESE
SACRED LILY'

'NIR'

'GRAND SOLEIL
D'OR'

'ZIVA'

'GALILEE'

VASE LIFE TRICKS

Paperwhites make a fantastic cut flower and look lovely mixed with forced branches, tulips, and amaryllises. For the longest vase life, be sure to cut flowers as soon as the individual blossoms start to open. Like other narcissus, paperwhites leak a toxic sap that will kill other flower types that are mixed with them in the vase. The best way to overcome this issue is to set your freshly harvested stems in a vase of cool water for 1 or 2 hours, to let the sap stop oozing, before combining them with other flowers. Do not recut the stems before mixing them with other blooms; that will expose the sap, and you'll need to start the whole process all over again.

Winter Projects

WELCOMING WREATH

I love the symbolism surrounding wreaths, including the circle of life, rebirth, generosity, and a sign of the approaching spring light—and there's nothing quite like the smell of freshly harvested evergreens to put me in the holiday spirit. A few weeks before holiday festivities begin, my family and I collect piles of ingredients for our winter wreath-making extravaganza. Then we spend our evenings by the fire, crafting dozens of wreaths for friends and clients. No two are ever the same. Once you understand the basic techniques for wreath making, the possibilities are limitless. If you've never made a wreath before, you're in for a treat. But I warn you, the process can become quite addicting, and you'll likely end up with a wall covered with evergreen halos before you know it. When you gather all of the ingredients that you'll be working with, be sure to include a wide variety of contrasting evergreen foliage—I like to use at least 6 to 8 different kinds—along with some unusual textural elements and fun little surprises like pinecones and berries.

YOU WILL NEED

Pruners

Wire cutters

1 spool of green, 22-gauge floral or paddle wire

One 14-inch (35-cm) wire wreath frame

At least 90 stems of assorted evergreens in 6- to 8-inch (15- to 20-cm) lengths

Optional: 3 to 6 pinecones in varying sizes; clusters of berries such as privet, holly, and ivy; and textural elements, including wheat, filbert catkins, and moss-covered twigs

1 Make 12 to 15 mixed evergreen bundles. For each bundle, cut 7 stems that are 6 to 8 inches (15 to 20 cm) long, and wrap the base of the stems together with wire. These will become the foundation of your wreath. Be sure to place the more basic evergreens at the back of the bundle and concentrate the unique, contrasting, and unusual elements on the front of the bundle.

2 Lay a bundle of greens on your wreath frame and secure it to the frame with a few wraps of floral wire.

3 Move a few inches down the frame and wire on your next bundle, making sure to keep the greenery facing the same direction as the last, hiding the wired ends under foliage as you go.

4 Continue this process until the entire frame is covered in greens.

5 Add the special little touches of pinecones, berries, and dried grains that will really make your finished wreath pop. Cluster these specialty elements together for greater impact and wire them onto the wreath. Mist twice daily if kept in a warm room.

INDOOR GARDEN

As winter draws to a close, I find that my anticipation for spring grows with every passing day. I eagerly watch the garden for signs of life and look for creative ways to cultivate a little dose of the spring garden indoors. I find that the smell of the fresh earth combined with the color of forced branches and bulbs satisfies my craving. Each winter I recreate a corner of my spring garden in an indoor vignette made up of a collection of potted bulbs, flowering branches, and fresh flowers. I save my very favorite fancy containers with piecrust edges and footed bases just for this use. When placed near a bright window, this simple project will have you feeling as if spring is right around the corner. The bulbs must be planted weeks in advance (depending on variety) of completing the arrangement. It can take a week or so for the branches to start flowering, and the bulbs may not bloom precisely on the same schedule, so while you wait, the small vases of blooming flowers will tide you over. If carefully tended, this indoor garden can carry you from midwinter to when the first flowers begin to unfold outdoors.

I often grab some bunches of tulips from the corner market and mix them in among the pots while the display is unfolding. Additionally, I pull new pots of bulbs from my stash in the basement every week and swap them with any that have passed their prime, so that I can stagger their flowering as well. And once my hellebores and snowdrops emerge outside, I replace the store-bought blooms with a few stems from my garden.

YOU WILL NEED

3 to 5 terra-cotta pots in varying sizes

One 1- to 2-foot (30- to 60-cm) tall vase, preferably clear glass

One or two 6- to 8-inch (15- to 20-cm) tall glass vases

Pruners to use as needed while arranging

Bulbs such as amaryllises and paperwhites

7 to 10 plum branches in bud, ready for forcing, cut so that they're 2 to 3 times the tall vase's height

1 or 2 bunches of flowers such as tulips or hellebores

1 Plant the bulbs in the terra-cotta pots, following the methods described earlier (see pages 269 and 291).

2 Fill the vases with water mixed with floral preservative. Place the tall vase at the back of the display and fill it with the plum branches.

3 Arrange the flowers in the shorter vases and the pots of bulbs in front.

299

4 Water the potted bulbs regularly to encourage vigorous growth. To keep the show going for as long as possible, replace spent branches with fresh ones so there is always a vase in bloom and one just about to explode.

LUSH GARLAND

A rope of fresh garland attached to a banister, draped over a mantel, or running down the center of a dining table is a quick and easy way to transform a space into a festive holiday wonderland. The piney scent paired with vibrant colors always makes for a memorable display.

At the most basic level, you're creating tiny bundles of greens, then attaching them to a rope, to create a thick, abundant evergreen garland. From there, you can customize your garland in any way you like. Aim for a variety of evergreens in contrasting colors and textures. I especially love pine, cedar, and Fraser fir. Be sure to harvest plenty, because these will become the base of your garland. Also round up some elements with unusual textures and colors, such as dried grains, little pinecones, winter berries like privet, dried fruit, and interesting twigs like filbert or red twig dogwood for added interest.

YOU WILL NEED

Garden gloves

Pruners

Wire cutters

Thick sisal twine or thin, natural-colored rope

1 spool of green 22-gauge floral or paddle wire

125 stems of varied evergreens (6 to 8 different types)

36 stems of textural elements, such as twigs, berries, pinecones, and/or dried grains

1 Cut your evergreen and textural branches down into 6- to 8-inch (15- to 20-cm) lengths. Sort the different elements into baskets or bins by type so that they stay organized and are easy to access.

2 Determine how long you want your garland to be, then cut a length of sisal twine a few feet longer than that. Once you start working, make sure to leave 12 to 18 inches (30 to 46 cm) of twine free at each end—this is how you'll hang it once it's finished. Place the twine on a flat surface, preferably at waist level.

3 Gather a bundle of 5 to 7 stems of evergreens and line up the ends. Lay them against the twine with tips pointing in the same direction, and tightly wrap the wire around both the greens and the twine, at least 4 or 5 times per bundle.

4 Continue to wire on bundles of greens, using 3 evenly spaced bundles per foot (30 cm). Overlap the ends as you go to hide the twine and wire; there's no need to cut the wire between each bundle. Once you reach your desired length, fully secure the wire by twisting or tying it to the last bundle so that all of your hard work doesn't accidentally come apart once you move the garland.

5 Punctuate your garland with bundles of textural elements—I use 2 evenly spaced bundles per foot (30 cm) on top of the greens, but you can customize your creation in any way that looks good to you.

6 If you want to add any larger elements like pinecones or big clusters of berries, attach them separately with wire to the finished garland. Mist your garland with water every day to help prolong its life. A fresh garland will do well for a couple of weeks in a cool room before it starts dropping needles; in a warm space, this will happen faster. If you want to display the garland through the entire holiday season, create a fresh one every 2 weeks.

RESOURCES

Though there are many sources for the following items, the ones listed here are my favorites.

A.M. LEONARD
www.amleo.com
Tools and supplies, including Atlas 370 nitrile gloves and the hori hori knife.

B&D LILIES
www.bdlilies.com
Mail-order nursery offering one of the best selections of lily bulbs on the market.

BRENT AND BECKY'S BULBS
http://brentandbeckysbulbs.com
Huge selection of spring-, summer-, and winter-flowering bulbs.

CAMPO DE' FIORI
http://campodefiori.com
Great source for specialty terra-cotta pots and planters.

DAN'S DAHLIAS
www.shop.dansdahlias.com
Offers over 300 varieties of top-quality dahlia tubers.

DAVID AUSTIN ROSES LIMITED
www.davidaustinroses.com
A great source for bare-root English garden roses.

DRIPWORKS
www.dripworks.com
Irrigation supplies, including drip tape and earth staples.

FARMHOUSE POTTERY
www.farmhousepottery.com
Great source for unique, handcrafted pottery vases.

FLORET FARM
www.floretflowers.com
Our online shop stocks the majority of the seeds, bulbs, and dahlias featured in this book along with the Farmer-Florist tool belt, flower snips, and pruners.

FORESTFARM
www.forestfarm.com
Mail-order source offering hundreds of hard-to-find potted perennials, shrubs, trees, and vines.

GARDEN VALLEY RANCH
www.gardenvalley.com
Mail-order nursery offering a large selection of bare-root roses.

GARDENER'S EDGE
www.gardenersedge.com
Root trainers.

GROWING SOLUTIONS
www.growingsolutions.com
Compost tea supplies and equipment.

JAMALI GARDEN
www.jamaligarden.com
Great source for unique vases and flower-arranging supplies, including floral preservative, bind wire, floral adhesive clay (Sure-Stik), floral tape/stem wrap, Oasis waterproof floral tape, rose thorn stripper, and water tubes.

JOHNNY'S SELECTED SEEDS
www.johnnyseeds.com
A wonderful mail-order source for seed-starting equipment, landscape fabric, flower netting, season extension supplies, hoop-house-making kits, specialty tools, natural fertilizers, and insect repellents.

KING'S MUMS
www.kingsmums.com
Mail-order nursery offering hundreds of heirloom chrysanthemum varieties.

LOWE'S
www.lowes.com
BernzOmatic propane torch for burning planting holes in landscape fabric.

RENEE'S GARDEN SEEDS
www.reneesgarden.com
Offers a large selection of cut flower seeds.

SAVE ON CRAFTS
www.save-on-crafts.com
Floral wire, flower frogs, paddle wire, and wire wreath frames.

SWAN ISLAND DAHLIAS
www.dahlias.com
Mail-order nursery offering hundreds of top-quality dahlia tubers.

THOMPSON & MORGAN
www.thompson-morgan.com
Offers an incredible selection of cut flower seeds.

UMASS SOIL AND PLANT TISSUE TESTING LAB
soiltest.umass.edu
Mail-order soil testing laboratory.

ACKNOWLEDGMENTS

Erin Benzakein

Making this book was an enormous undertaking that consumed the better part of a year of my family's life. Without the help and support of the following people, I would never have been able to bring it to life. First, I would like to acknowledge my incredible husband, Chris. His unwavering belief in my ability to write this book and his loving support are what kept me going through the many late nights, early mornings, and weekends filled with writing and photo shoots. My kids, Elora and Jasper, were so supportive of my following this dream, even though it meant spending nearly every weekend for a year away from them and in front of the computer. My mom, Cherie, took the most amazing care of the kids while I was focused on the project and helped keep my head in the game when the pressure of it all felt like too much to bear. My dear friend Jill sat with me during the earliest stages of the project and guided it from an abstract dream into an actual book. Without her wisdom and steady encouragement throughout the process, I never would have made it through. Team Floret held down the fort and kept things running smoothly on the farm while I was away. My wonderful friend Nina came from Vermont to help with the shoots and turned the overwhelming task of capturing all the details into a fun adventure. Michèle Waite's

images are more beautiful than I could have ever imagined, and her willingness to squeeze this project into her already full life was such a blessing. Julie Chai, the best editor and guide anyone could ever ask for, taught me so much about life, speaking my truth, and writing through our time working together. My agent is Leslie Jonath; her wise counsel, enthusiasm for the project, and faith in me were priceless. Laura Lee Mattingly, Anne Kenady, Rachel Hiles, Deanne Katz, and the Chronicle Books team, thank you for your expert insights and helping us bring this book to life. John and Toni Christenson generously let us take over their schoolhouse and nursery when we needed a pretty backdrop for photos, and the kind folks at Farmhouse Pottery sent the most beautiful vessels in which to create the arrangements. Geraldine from Northfield Farm let us have free rein of her field during the height of peony season, and Gordon Skagit Farms allowed us to capture magical photos of their farm during peak apple blossom and pumpkin season. Lastly, a massive thank-you to all of the wonderful Floret supporters who follow along on social media, read our blog, buy our flowers, and attend our workshops and who so generously helped me get clear on what to include in these pages. This book is for you!

305

Julie Chai

My grandma Frances Greth was the first gardener I knew, and her plot was packed with treasures including a spectacular rose bed, an abundance of bulbs, flowering trees, and in summer, a long row of luscious tomatoes. She cared about surrounding herself with natural beauty, and I'm forever grateful to her for showing me the importance of that. Beauty can uplift, inspire, and transform everyone who sees it, and anyone who's ever received a gift of freshly clipped flowers from a friend's backyard knows that even the simplest bouquet can lift your spirits every time you look at it. So, having the opportunity to work with Erin Benzakein on a book that gives aspiring growers the knowledge to raise their own abundant gardens—and fill the world with gorgeous blooms—has been a privilege and a pleasure. Erin, thank you for inviting me to join in such a personal project and trusting me with your work. I'm continually inspired by your work ethic, bigheartedness, and dedication to doing whatever it

took to make this book one that empowers everyone who reads it. I'm a fan not only of your floral designs, but also of your sincere intention to help others capture more beauty in each moment. Leslie Jonath, Erin's agent and my dear friend, a thousand thanks for connecting us. Your creativity, enthusiasm, and generosity are unmatched. Laura Lee Mattingly, Anne Kenady, Rachel Hiles, and Deanne Katz at Chronicle Books, I'm grateful for your thoughtful guidance, and all the time and care you put into making this title so stunning. My parents, Phyllis and Hi-Dong Chai, and my husband, George Lee: thank you for being so supportive of this project in every way. You cheered me on while I was a sleep-deprived new mom trying to meet deadlines, and your eternal optimism and sense of humor helped me keep things moving along. To our son, Ellis, whose curiosity, enthusiasm, and sheer delight in life bring me joy every single day: You are my favorite sprout of all.

INDEX

306

308